Mi

Peer Assessment as a Lear

Minjeong Kim

Peer Assessment as a Learning Method

The Effects of the Assessor and Assessee's Role on Metacognitive Awareness, Performance, and Attitude

VDM Verlag Dr. Müller

Imprint

Bibliographic information by the German National Library: The German National Library lists this publication at the German National Bibliography; detailed bibliographic information is available on the Internet at http://dnb.d-nb.de.

Any brand names and product names mentioned in this book are subject to trademark, brand or patent protection and are trademarks or registered trademarks of their respective holders. The use of brand names, product names, common names, trade names, product descriptions etc. even without a particular marking in this works is in no way to be construed to mean that such names may be regarded as unrestricted in respect of trademark and brand protection legislation and could thus be used by anyone.

Cover image: www.purestockx.com

Publisher:
VDM Verlag Dr. Müller Aktiengesellschaft & Co. KG
Dudweiler Landstr. 125 a, 66123 Saarbrücken, Germany
Phone +49 681 9100-698, Fax +49 681 9100-988, Email: info@vdm-verlag.de

Produced in USA and UK by:
Lightning Source Inc., La Vergne, Tennessee, USA
Lightning Source UK Ltd., Milton Keynes, UK

ISBN: 978-3-8364-3665-6

TABLE OF CONTENTS

LIST OF TABLES

LIST OF FIGURES

ABSTRACT

Considerable attention has been directed toward the value of peer assessment where learning is enhanced through maximizing the opportunities for students to share their work with others in the assessment process. Although previous research has shown the effectiveness of peer assessment, very little work has been done to investigate the effects of the different types of learner roles in peer assessment on learning. Therefore, this study investigated the effects of the Assessor and Assessee's role on preservice teachers' metacognitive awareness, performance, and attitude in a technology-related design task.

This study examined three specific questions:

Question 1. What are the comparative effects of the Assessor's role and Assessee's role on metacognitive awareness, performance, and attitude?

Question 2. Does the role combination (playing both Assessor's role and Assessee's role simultaneously) improve learners' metacognitive awareness, performance, and attitude to a greater degree than either of the roles alone or neither role?

Question 3. Are there any relationships between the quality of peer feedback and Assessees' metacognitive awareness, performance, and attitude?

Eighty-two students (preservice teachers) from four sections of an Introduction to Educational Technology course at the Florida State University participated in this study. The four sections were randomly assigned to four conditions (Assessor-only role condition, Assessee-only role condition, Both-roles condition, and control condition.

At first, the participants submitted a technology-related design assignment (concept mapping by Inspiration) to the instructor. After gathering students' concept map, the researcher randomly assigned assessee's concept maps to peer assessors. Student assessors received a peer's concept map and assessed it for 20 minutes. After completing peer assessment, student assessors submitted their assessment form to the instructor. The instructor delivered the peer feedback to the assessees. Then, the assessees had an opportunity to reflect peer feedback by filling out back-feedback (feedback on feedback) form. Immediately following the peer assessment activities, the instructor returned the draft concept map to the students and asked them to revise it based on the experience of peer assessment. After they finishing revising, students resubmitted the final concept map to instructor, which served as the posttest for the study. After submitting this final concept map assignment, students completed a metacognitive awareness questionnaire and an attitude survey.

To compare the main effects of the two different types of role (assessor's role & assessee's role), a two-factor MANOVA was employed. In addition, to compare the mean difference across conditions, a one-factor MANOVA was employed. For all tests, the alpha level was set at .05.

The results indicated that the Assessee's role was helpful for students to enhance metacognitive awareness on their own learning and to promote their performance, while the assessor's role did not show significant effectiveness. This may be attributed to the back-feedback activity, which seemed to help the Assessees internalize and reflect upon the peer feedback.

With respect to the effects of the combination role (playing both roles: assessor's role + assessee's role), the Both-roles condition did not always outperform the Assessor-only role condition or Assessee-only role condition. Contrary to what had been hypothesized, the one role only conditions sometimes outperformed the Both-roles condition. The results of this study illustrated that simply playing two different roles at a time does not always guarantee better effects of peer assessment than playing only one role. Even when students play only one role during peer assessment, they can have benefits of peer assessment for their learning.

The back-feedback score and Assessee's performance was significantly associated, but negatively. It may be explained by the degree of students' understanding of the assessment criteria and the requirements of the assignment. By giving the Assessees the opportunity to critique their peer's (Assessor's) feedback, it seems to have empowered them to have better understand the criteria and prove their own performance.

The findings of this study suggest instructional implications for those who want to employ peer assessment through providing examples regarding the effectiveness of well-developed assessment criteria and instructional activities, particularly the back-feedback activity. Due to the lack of fully randomized design and the short treatment time, the results and interpretation are tentative. Further studies to verify the results are recommended.

student-centred learning require alternative assessment techniques.

CHAPTER 1
INTRODUCTION

Context of Problem

Assessment is a critical aspect of education and the importance and prevalence of student-centered learning require alternative assessment techniques to evaluate learning and teaching. Many innovative assessment approaches thus have been proposed and they promote the integration of assessment and learning by increasing student involvement in the assessment activities (Sluijsmans, Brand-Gruwel, vanMerrienboer, & Bastiens, 2003). From the perspective of those approaches, students are considered active agents who share responsibilities, reflect, collaborate and conduct a continuous dialogue with the instructor and/or peers. In addition, assessment is not entirely about grading students' work, rather assessment is used to monitor students' progress and improve their learning activities by engaging them in the assessment activities. Student involvement in assessment has been increasing extensively in higher educational setting in diverse fields such as writing, business, science, engineering, and medicine (Falchikov, 1995; Freeman, 1995; Rada, Acquah, Baker, & Ramsey, 1993; Strachan & Wilcox, 1996). More recently researchers have proposed the idea of using assessment as a learning method (Boud, 1995; Gayo-Avello & Fernandes-Cuervo, 2003; R. Johnson, 1999; McDowell, 1995; Purchase, 2000; Rust, Price, & O'Donovan, 2003; Smyth, 2004).

Among various types of student involvement in assessment, considerable attention has been directed toward the value of peer assessment because learning is enhanced through

1

maximizing the opportunities for students to discuss their work with others in the assessment process (Boud, 1995). In peer assessment, students use their knowledge and skills to review, clarify, and correct others' work. When playing a role of assessor, students are involved in reviewing, summarizing, clarifying, giving feedback, diagnosing misconceived knowledge, identifying missing knowledge, and considering deviations from the ideal (Topping, 1998). These are all cognitively and metacognitively demanding activities that could help to consolidate, reinforce, and deepen understanding in the assessor. Moreover, assessed work with feedback can help students articulate the attributes of good and poor performance and promote their thinking and learning. Therefore, it is often claimed that peer assessment encourages students to become critical, independent learners as they become more familiar with the application of assessment criteria and develop a clearer concept of the topic being reviewed (Falchikov, 1995; Searby & Ewers, 1997).

In addition, peer assessment encourages students to develop responsibilities and a sense of ownership for their peers' learning (Dochy, Segers, & Sluijsmans, 1999; Orsmond, Merry, & Reiling, 1996; Topping, Smith, Swanson, & Elliot, 2000). It is also argued that this cooperative approach to learning is further enhanced when the process involves group submissions or group assessment (Ballantyne, Hughies, & Mylonas, 2002). For example, Topping and his colleagues (2000) suggest that peer assessment has the potential to improve students' verbal communication and negotiation skills, as well as their ability to give and receive criticism.

In contrast, some authors have reported disadvantages or problems with their implementation of peer assessment (Brindley & Scoffield, 1998; Cheng & Warren, 1997; Falchikov, 1995; McDowell, 1995; Mowl & Pain, 1995). Poor performers might not accept peer feedback as accurate. Students might not be willing to accept any responsibility for assessing their peers. One of the consequence of the above findings is that students often lack confidence in both their own and their peers' abilities as assessors (Ballantyne et al., 2002). Such lack of confidence may result in low reliability and validity of peer assessment.

However, as Devenney (1989) indicated, the role and function of peer assessment might differ from that of instructor assessment, so high reliability might not be necessary. This is particularly true if we consider the purpose of peer assessment. Peer assessment can be classified by its purpose as either formative or summative peer assessment. Whereas summative peer assessment is to determine success or failure only after the event like instructor's assessment, formative peer assessment has often used to improve learning while it is happening. Specifically, formative peer assessment is intended to help students plan their own learning, identify their own strengths and weaknesses, target areas for remedial action, and develop metacognitive skills and transferable skills (Boud, 1990; Brown & Knight, 1994). Formative peer assessment focuses mainly on improvement learner's learning by stimulating learner's reflection through peer assessment activities rather than on accurate-scoring and high quality feedback itself. With such characteristics, formative peer assessment has been often used as a learning method.

There is an increasing demand for formative peer assessment in teacher education as the technique fits in well with the latest view on education of preservice teachers (Sluijsmans et al., 2003). This view maintains that preservice teachers debate with peers about required teaching skills and their implications in real class situations. Experience of peer assessment may benefit preservice teachers in the following two ways. Such experience could enhance their awareness of the benefits of peer assessment (Bangert, 1995) and thus lead them to be more likely to apply the technique to their future practice. The other advantage is that such first-hand experience could assist preservice teachers in designing and developing assessments for their future students.

Problem Statement

Examinations of our current understanding of peer assessment generated from prior studies indicate the need for a richer understanding of peer assessment. Although peer assessment has been found to be beneficial to students learning, the researchers have not provided strong evidence to establish an unambiguous relationship between peer assessment and learning improvement. This is particularly true in the area of the effect of peer assessment when learners take different roles (e.g.,the role of assessor or assessee) during an peer assessment activity. For instance, much of the research studies in the past decades have focused on the beneficial aspects of peer assessment acquired by taking the assessor's role (Blom & Poole, 2004; Kim, 2003; Sluijsmans et al., 2003; Topping et al., 2000; Tsai, Lin, & Yhan, 2002). Such studies have significantly added to our understanding of how student assessors learn and what

3

benefits they acquire through peer assessment, but they did not address whether similar process and benefits would occur if students play the role of assessee.

In addition, although much research has been conducted in various fields (Butcher, Stefani, & Tariq, 1995; Ewers & Searby, 1997; Mowl & Pain, 1995; Rushton, Ramsey, & Rada, 1993; Topping, 1998), far less research has been performed in the teacher education field and many questions are to be answered. For example, does a peer assessment activity change preservice teachers' perspective of the value of peer assessment? Does a peer assessment activity promote preservice teachers' self-reported regulatory skills for doing a task? Does playing the role of assessor promote preservice teachers' learning performance? Does playing the role of the assessee impact preservice teachers' attitude toward peer assessment and the subject? These questions have not been fully explored in previous peer assessment research, particularly when the students play different roles during a peer assessment activity.

Purpose of the Study

The purpose of this study is to examine the effects of peer assessment on preservice teachers' metacognitive awareness, performance, and attitude in a technology-related design task when learners take different roles. Specifically, the study attempts to gather empirical evidence on the effect of two different types of learner's role in peer assessment – the assessor's role and assessee's role – on metacognitive awareness (i.e., changes in perspective of the value of peer assessment and self-reported regulatory skills for doing a task), performance (i.e., quality of the technology-related design task), and learner attitude (i.e., motivation measured with four sub-constructs of attention, relevance, confidence, and satisfaction).

4

assessee as mirror
and as mirror.

Research Questions

In this section, definition of the terms for this study will be presented first to set the stage for the research questions of the study. The key terms in this study are "peer assessment," "type of learner's role," "Assessor's role," and "Assessee's role." They are defined as follows:

1. **Peer assessment** is often used to determine the amount, level, value or worth of peer's work. In this case, peer assessment focuses on the product and outcome of learning rather than processes or procedures (Topping & Ehly, 1998). However, peer assessment in this study is considered to be a formative-purpose learning activity that is to support their peers by giving useful feedback and to help themselves reflect upon their own learning by assessing a peer's work or receiving peer feedback.

2. **Type of learner's role** is what role learner plays during peer assessment. In this study, the types of learner's role include: (a) assessor's role, and (b) assessee's role.
    (a) **Assessor's role** is a type of learner's role in peer assessment where learners assess peer's work and give feedback.
    (b) **Assessee's role** is a type of learner's role in peer assessment where learners receive peer feedback. In this study, the learners who play an assessee's role will have a chance to write back-feedback (feedback-on-feedback).

With the given the definition, this study will focus on how the Assessor's role and Assessee's role affect preservice teachers' metacognitive awareness, performance, and attitude in technology-related design task. In attempting to answer this general question, this study specifically will explore the following questions.

1. What are the comparative effects of the Assessor's role and Assessee's role on metacognitive awareness, performance, and attitude?
2. Does the role combination (playing both Assessor's role and Assessee's role simultaneously) improve learners' metacognitive awareness, performance, and attitude to a greater degree than either of the role alone or neither role?

3. Are there any relationships between the quality of peer feedback and Assessees' metacognitive awareness, performance, and attitude?

Significance of the Study

The prevalence of peer assessment speaks to the value of this study which seeks to further enrich our understanding of peer assessment. The present study will contribute to research on peer assessment in several ways.

First, the potentiality of peer assessment as a learning method has not received adequate attention. This is evident in the small number of studies on peer assessment as a learning method. Thus, this study has the potential to provide guidelines for practitioners who are interested in using peer assessment as a learning method.

Second, this study may make contributions to the theoretical perspectives of peer assessment. Many of the studies on peer assessment consider social constructivism – the joint construction of knowledge through discourse and other interactivity – as an appropriate theoretical framework (Falchikov, 2003; McLuckie & Topping, 2004; Topping, 1998). However, this study uses a new theoretical perspective, self-regulated learning process, as the primary framework to examine peer assessment. In other words, peer assessment process is considered to be a self-regulated learning process in this study. Students set goals to pursue and they work on a variety of tasks such as assessing peer's work, giving feedback, receiving feedback, and revising their work based on external feedback (peer feedback) and internal feedback (self-monitoring and self-reflection).

In addition, most of the studies on formative peer assessment have been conducted in the field of writing (in this case, peer assessment is often called peer review), although a variety of trials of peer assessment were in other disciplines. As it is encouraged that preservice teachers debate with peers about required teaching skills and their implications in real class situations and they improve their own learning and teaching based on such feedback, studies that investigate the use of formative peer assessment will be of interest to researchers and practitioners in teacher education field as well.

6

Thinking about the way you think.

Finally, results from this study may lead to give prescriptive instructional strategies by comparing directly the effects of the two types of learner's role on various dependent variables. For example, if the students who played the role of assessor show significantly higher metacognitive awareness than others, we can say that Assessor's role (assessing something and giving feedback) may be effective to promote metacognitive awareness in preservice teachers' technology-related design task. On the contrary, if the students who played a role of assessee show significantly higher performance than others, we can say that Assessee's role (receiving peer feedback) may be effective in preservice teachers' technology-related design task performance. The results of the study are likely to provide practical guidelines by suggesting specific instructional strategies for practitioners who are interested in using peer assessment as a learning method.

CHAPTER II
REVIEW OF LITERATURE

Introduction

The essential assumption underlying this study is that peer assessment can be used as a learning method to facilitate learners' cognitive and metacognitive skills. For the assessor, peer assessment can provide the opportunities for reflection through the experience of assessing. On the other hand, for the assessee, peer assessment can provide potentially useful feedback. Based on this assumption, the chapter will contain the following four sections.

The first section will serve to ground the essential assumption of this study, the use of peer assessment as a learning method. Specifically, this section will present the characteristics of formative peer assessment as a learning method by reviewing common stages of formative peer assessment.

The second section will discuss the theoretical background of peer assessment. This section will start with defining the learner's role in peer assessment, and it is followed by a review of the theoretical foundations of peer assessment from the perspective of different learners' role (Assessor or Assessee). From the perspective of the assessor in peer assessment, the related theoretical foundations include 1) constructionism (learning by design), and 2) role model theory. From the perspective of the assessee, 1) scaffolding, and 2) behavioristic approach on feedback will be reviewed as the theoretical foundations. Finally, 1) cooperative learning, and 2) self-regulated learning will be presented as the theoretical foundations for the potential effect of the combination of two different roles (Assessor's role and Assessee's role) on promoting reflective learning.

The third section will review previous studies on the effects of peer assessment. The section in particular will focus on how learners obtain different benefits by playing different roles (Assessor or Assessee) in peer assessment. The purpose of this section is to provide an overview of the issues that have been studied so far. At the end of the review, the limitations of previous studies will be discussed.

The fourth section will describe the research questions and hypotheses of this study, and how they address the limitations of previous studies.

Peer Assessment as a Learning Method

Peer assessment can be classified into formative peer assessment and summative peer assessment. Summative peer assessment occurs at the end of an event to determine whether pre-determined objectives have been achieved. In contrast, formative peer assessment can be used to improve learning while it is happening in order to maximize successful learning. Thus formative assessment seems likely to be most helpful if the purpose of the assessment is to assist learning. Unlike summative assessment where a quantitative mark or grade is given with little explanation and few chances for further improvement, formative peer assessment usually provides rich and detailed qualitative feedback and learners have detailed information about the strengths and weaknesses (Topping et al, 2000).

Formative assessment thus has been used as a learning method rather than an assessment tool (Keig, 2000; Orsmond et al, 2002; Topping et al., 2000). Currently there is no model acknowledged by researchers in the field that explicitly expresses the process of peer assessment as a learning method. Many aspects of peer assessment are unique to each individual study and they differ in assessment task, task level, product, subject area, or a combination of two or more aspects. However, one aspect consistent across researchers in peer assessment is the stages that learners go through when peer assessment is used as a learning method to improve students'

9

learning: planning, assessing, receiving peer feedback, reviewing, and revising (Kim, 2004). More detailed description of each stage will be described in the next section.

Stages of Formative Peer Assessment

1. Preparation/Planning. The first stage that learners in formative purpose peer assessment is to consider the objectives and purposes of the assessment task as well as the course itself (Boud, 1995; Topping et al., 2000). During the process of planning, assessors set their assessment goals based on identified objectives and purposes of the assessment. They then organize their ideas and set procedural and substantive goals.

One of the important tasks in the planning stage is to set assessment criteria. Assessment criteria are critical as they make tacit knowledge explicit to others (Rust et al., 2003) and at the same time serve to improve the quality of peer feedback. In addition, they make students aware of their achievement and ability to understand assessment feedback (Bloxham & West, 2004). Recently some researchers have reported the use of student-derived grading criteria and their effectiveness in peer assessment (Orsmond, Merry, & Reiling, 2000; Orsmond et al., 2002). As students-derived criteria help students more actively involved in learning, using peer assessment as an effective formative assessment tool can be an effective instructional strategy.

2. Conducting (assessing peer's work). Peer assessment provides an opportunity for students to view and critique peer's work, techniques, ideas and abilities. Conducting peer assessment encourages students to learn from both the mistakes and exemplary performances of their peers (Race, 1998). In addition, students' skills of critiquing or evaluating their own work (self-assessment) improve as a result of the experience of peer assessment (Tower & Broadfoot, 1992). They may acquire new strategies or knowledge for task performance or fine-tune existing strategies or knowledge. Such process resembles that of 'learning by design' in that students actively use their prior knowledge to assess a peer's work and construct new knowledge structure based on the peer assessment experience.

3. Receiving peer feedback. After peer's products are reviewed, the products are usually returned back to the authors with peer feedback. Peer feedback is peer-monitored data that can be a time-efficient and resource-efficient procedure for more frequent data collection (Topping & Ehly, 1998). Despite those advantages, peer feedback has some limitations in terms of its validity and reliability. One of the most common issues on peer feedback is the quality of peer feedback. Many peer assessment studies have dealt with the validity or reliability issues of peer feedback by comparing peer feedback with instructor feedback (Falchikov, 1995; Lin, Liu, & Yuan, 2001; Orsmond et al., 2000).

comparing peer feedback with instructor feedback

Common characteristics of those studies are they consider peer assessment as an alternative assessment tool rather than a learning method. In other words, those studies focus on the score or grade of peer assessment in order to use it instead of as an alternative to instructor's score or grade. That is the primary reason why the issue of reliability and validity of peer assessment are critically important in those cases.

Although the quality of peer feedback remains important when peer assessment is used as a learning method, this approach emphasizes the role of feedback as a scaffolding tool rather than as an assessment itself. Therefore, formative peer assessment often uses qualitative feedback to give formative information for students' learning (e.g., what is weakness? what should be improved?) in addition to a score or grade

4. Reviewing/Reflection. After finishing assessment task, students (Assessors) are encouraged to reflect on their own approaches to the assessment task (Dochy et al., 1999). At the same time, peer assessment enables students (Assessee) to appreciate why and how grades are awarded (Brindley & Scoffield, 1998). The reviewing stage emphasizes on self-assessment through reflection. Many studies have been reported that peer assessment is highly associated with self-assessment (Blom & Poole, 2004; Dochy et al., 1999; Lejk & Wyvill, 2001).

The reviewing stage is the key feature that differentiates between peer assessment as an assessment and peer assessment as a learning method. Peer assessment as a learning method is not a linear learning process but iterative learning processes based on feedback system. When engaged in peer assessment as a learning method, students set goals for the assessment or their own learning and identify strategies or tactics to help them achieve the goals. In addition, they monitor their own progress toward those goals, and adjust their strategies or even their goals based on feedback.

5. Revising. If peer assessment is completed immediately after the reviewing stage without further action, we cannot recognize what is improved and what are in need of improvement. Formative peer assessment emphasizes not only adjusting learning strategies or goals based on feedback, but also making changes to the product. Such an iterative characteristic is a key feature of peer assessment as a learning method.

The following figure (Figure 2.1) shows the common stages of peer assessment and the sequence of the process.

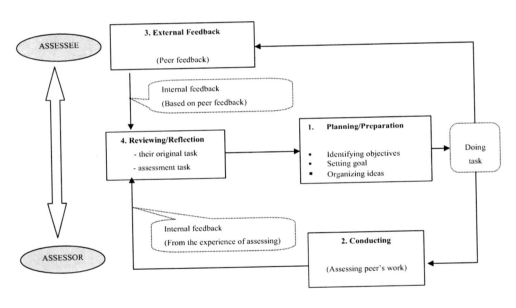

Figure 2.1 General process model of peer assessment as a learning method

As the Figure 2.1 shows, peer assessment as a learning method is an iterative process. Unlike traditional assessment, it starts from the planning stage and it does not end with assesses receiving feedback from the assessors. Learners (both Assessors and Assessees) are supposed to reflect upon their own learning and assessment process. They then are given opportunities to revise their original products or even goals based on internal and external feedback. These processes of peer assessment as a learning method resemble those in self-regulated learning. Therefore, this study will approach peer assessment as a learning method from the perspective of self-regulated learning.

Summary

Peer assessment as a learning method is usually used for formative purposes rather than summative grading or scoring. Therefore, open or qualitative feedback is more valuable than a simple numerical score. However, as feedback in general terms is not very helpful for students, detailed criteria are often constructed to generate structured formative feedback. Another difference between peer assessment as a learning method and peer assessment as an assessment tool is the assessment process. When peer assessment is employed only as an assessment tool, receiving feedback is the final stage (See Table 2.1). Peer assessment as a learning method, on the other hand, starts from planning stage followed by conducting stage, receiving feedback stage, reflection stage, and revising stage iteratively. The reflection and revising stages, which are absent in peer assessment as an assessment, tool are critical components in peer assessment as a learning method and they aim to improve students' learning by engaging them to reflect.

Table 2.1 Different type of peer assessment

		Peer assessment as an alternative assessment	Peer assessment as a learning method
Purpose		Replace instructor assessment	Learning method
Commonly expressed outcome		Score, grade	Open feedback, score or grade with specific criteria
Activities in each stage	1. Planning	Instructor plans assessment goal, procedure and criteria	Learner plans his/her own assessment or learning goal
	2. Conducting	Activities for marking or grading	Activities for scaffolded learning
	3. Receiving	Receiving grade or score (Final stage)	Receiving peer feedback for revision
	4. Reviewing/ Reflection	N/A	Self-assessment through reflection
	5. Revising	N/A	Adjusting goals and learning strategies and making changes based on them
Structure		Linear	Iterative

Theoretical Background of Peer Assessment

One of the assumptions of this study is that the benefit of peer assessment may be differentiated by the role that learners play during peer assessment activities. Therefore, this section will review underlying theories related to the roles of learners. From the assessor's perspective (assessing and giving feedback), constructionism and role-model theory will be reviewed. From assessee's perspective (receiving peer feedback), behaviorism and scaffolding will be reviewed. Finally, cooperative learning and self-regulated leaning will be discussed in relation to the role of student as both assessor and assessee (when the student is both the Assessor and Assessee) (See Table 2.2).

Table 2.2 Theoretical background of peer assessment

	Underlying Theories	
	For individual learner	For social relationship
In general	▪ Self-regulated learning	▪ Cooperative learning
By learner's role		
Assessor's role	▪ Constructionism (learning by design)	▪ Role model theory
Assessee's role	▪ Behaviorist approach (feedback)	▪ Scaffolding

From Assessor's Perspective

In peer assessment, the main role of the assessor is to assess peer's work and give feedback. This study will review constructionism and role-model theory as theoretical frameworks in relation to student role as assessor. Constructionism addresses the student role as assessor in terms of individual learner's learning while role-model theory points our attention to social relationship involved when the student is in the role of assessor.

Constructionism (learning by design). Constructionism, a learning theory, argues that people learn best when they are active participants in design activities (Papert, 1993) and that these activities give them a greater sense of control over (and personal involvement in) the learning process (Resnick, Bruckman, & Martin, 1996). According to Kafai and Resnick (1996), students are particularly likely to construct new ideas when they are actively engaged in making some type of external artifact which they can reflect upon and share with others. This process, in constructionists' terms, is called "learning by design." It is an approach to learning in which students learn as a result of collaboratively engaging in design activities and reflecting appropriately on their experiences. Participants learn concepts by experiencing how those concepts work; they learn applicability of concepts by applying them to solving real-world problems; they learn problem-solving, decision-making, and collaborative skills by engaging in such activities that require them to use those skills.

The main purpose of a design task is to have students create a design product or artifact such as a piece of instruction method or learning method. One assumption underlying such projects is that the active use of prior domain knowledge and problem solving during design tasks will improve the acquisition of domain knowledge and facilitate the construction of new knowledge.

The perspective of learning by design has particular relevance to the student role as assessor. In peer assessment, assessors can benefit from being actively involved in assessment activities. During the assessment process, assessors actively use their prior knowledge to assess a peer's work and construct new knowledge based on the peer assessment experience.

Role-model theory. According to role-model theory, individuals taking specific roles will feel themselves constrained by the expectations of other people so that they would behave in particular ways (Goodlad & Hirst, 1989). For example, if a student is temporarily given the role of teacher, and put into interaction with other students, the student who plays a teacher's role will be constrained by the expectations of the other students. Thereby the student who plays a teacher's role will sympathize with the role of teacher and perhaps develop a deeper respect for learning.

Although there is no study on peer assessment based on role-model theory, much research on peer tutoring draws upon this model. For example, Garter (1971) described that students who were given the role of teacher acted like teachers and this led to improved behavior and attitude. In addition, the student who took a teacher's role found a meaningful use of the subject matter of his/her study.

This theory can be applicable to the role of assessor in peer assessment. If a student is temporarily given the role of assessor, and put into evaluating others' work, the assessors will be constrained by the expectations of assesses. The assessor will make every effort possible to conduct the assessment like teacher. In addition, this process can potentially improve the assessor's behavior, attitude, and his/her own learning as a result of this experience.

16

From Assessees's Perspective

In peer assessment, the major responsibility of the Assessee is to receive peer feedback. In this section, behaviorist approach to feedback and scaffolding as theoretical frameworks will be reviewed in relation to the student role as assessee. This section will describe a behaviorist approach to feedback with the focus on the individual learner's (Assessee's) learning. Additionally, scaffolding will be presented as an underlying theory from the perspective of social relationship.

Behaviorist approach to feedback. The basic idea of behaviorism on learning is that learning will be effective if every correct response is rewarded and the rewarded action serves as a stimulus to the learner to another step in learning. In peer assessment, Assessees can be guided by an assessor who presents correct feedback in a suitable order. Of course, peer feedback might be lower in quality than teacher feedback. However, one evident advantage is that peer feedback is usually more prompt and frequent than teacher feedback. In addition, efforts have been made to generate more accurate and helpful peer feedback including the use of more structured criteria (Bloxham & West, 2004; Miller, 2003).

In peer assessment, peer feedback can be a factor influencing affective well as cognitive dimensions of learning. For example, positive peer feedback can support the assessee's intrinsic motivation (Csikszentmihalyi, 1978) or self-attributions. For example, positive peer feedback can support assessee's intrinsic motivation (Csikszentmihalyi, 1978) or self-attributions (Dweck, 1975). In addition, peer feedback can assist self-regulated learning by cuing self-monitoring and engaging learners in other metacognitive process (Topping & Ehly, 1998).

Scaffolding. Learning and development are intertwined from the very beginning of a child's development (Vygotsky, Cole, John-Steiner, Scribner, & Souberman, 1978). At the center of learning and the developmental process is the concept of the zone of proximal development (ZPD): a distance between the actual and potential development of a learner with the assistance of others. The concept of ZPD supports the idea that effective learning requires support and guidance from a more capable peer. Researchers have suggested scaffolding as an instructional strategy to support intellectual development of learners in the zone of proximal development. Chi (1996), for instance, discriminated scaffolding from prompting. According to her definition, a prompt would include simple elucidative verbalizations such as "go on," "what comes next?" while scaffolding would include describing the problem to orient students to the significant features, suggesting a specific goal, and initiating a reasoning sequence. By providing scaffolding, the instructor or peer support learners of lower competency as they understand the world and construct knowledge.

In peer assessment, assesses can be supported with scaffolding to facilitate learning but they are not always supported by advanced peers (assessors). For the reason, many studies have reported the importance of development of assessment criteria for assessors (Miller, 2003; Orsmond et al., 2000, 2002; Woolf, 2004). Well-developed assessment criteria can increase the quality of peer feedback by providing a concrete structure for the assessment.

From Role Combination Perspective
(When the student plays both the Assessor's role and Assessee's role)

In general, students play two roles – the role of Assessor and Assessee - in peer assessment. They assess their peer's work and they also receive feedback from their peers. The following section will review self-regulated learning and cooperative learning as the theoretical frameworks for the two roles assumed by the students in peer assessment. Self-regulated learning speaks to individual learner's learning while cooperative learning addresses the issues related to the social relationship of the peers.

Self-regulated learning. Formative peer assessment resembles self-regulated learning in terms of learners' cognitive and metacognitive engagement in their own learning and self-oriented feedback loop. For the reason, this study approaches the peer assessment process from the perspective of self-regulated learning. For example, students have a clear understanding of the objectives of assessment and select goals to pursue in planning stage of peer assessment. Then, students work on a variety of tasks such as assessing peer's work, giving feedback, and receiving feedback. All of these activities are highly related with self-regulated learning by focusing feedback (either external or internal) that is essential to the development and execution of self-regulatory skills (Paris & Newman, 1990). Finally, students evaluate weaknesses and strengths on a given assessment task and their own product (Oldfield & MacAlpine, 1995), and revising their product bases on reflection and peer feedback that are filtered by a learner's belief system and understanding of goals of the task (Butler & Winne, 1995).

Therefore, well-developed peer assessment can be used as a tool to enhance students' self-regulated learning by providing the information on how to plan, allocate resources, seek help, evaluate their own performance, and revise and correct their own work.

Cooperative learning. As various peer assessment techniques used in group situation are based on the use of reciprocal relationships, collaborative learning and cooperative learning are thus relevant to peer assessment. The underlying premise for both collaborative and cooperative learning is constructivist theory which posits that knowledge is discovered and constructed by students and transformed into concepts to which students can relate. Then, the newly constructed knowledge is then reconstructed and expanded through new learning experiences. Learning and knowledge construction is a result of active participation by students. Constructivist theory fits well with formative peer assessment. In peer assessment, learning comes about through transactions among students and students learn to understand and appreciate different perspectives.

This study will approach peer assessment from the perspective of cooperative learning rather than that of collaborative learning, as there are differences between the two approaches. Although both cooperative learning and collaborative learning are about two or more people learning together, cooperative learning usually gives more emphasis on accomplishing a specific goal or developing an end product that is usually content specific (Panitz, 1997). In addition, cooperative learning is more directive than collaborative learning. In cooperative learning, system of governance is somewhat from the teacher (Panitz, 1997). Thus the role of instructor in peer assessment bears more similarity with that defined by cooperative learning. For example, teachers can implement peer assessment to help students achieve a specific learning goal. For the effective implementation of peer assessment, teacher should design peer assessment techniques and activities, and develop peer assessment criteria before they administrate peer assessment. Thus, though peer assessment is used a learning tool enhancing learner-centered learning, the role of instructor to ensure the successful implementation of peer assessment cannot be underestimated.

Furthermore, five basic elements in the procedure of cooperative learning identified by Johnson and his colleagues (1991) ideas are also applicable to peer assessment: 1) Positive interdependence, 2) individual accountability, 3) face-to-face interaction, 4) interpersonal and small group skills, and 5) group processing. In order for peer assessment to be successful, mechanisms that reflect the five elements in cooperative learning should be built into the process to maximize the effects of peer assessment. For instance, if students perceive that they need each other to achieve a specific learning goal, they would do their best when assessing peer's work. And, if they can have some time to discuss how well they are achieving their goals through peer assessment, it would be very helpful for their reflection.

Effects of Peer Assessment

Many previous studies have investigated the effects of peer assessment (Ballantyne et al., 2002; Orsmond et al., 2000, 2002; Smyth, 2004). The major effects of peer assessment that previous studies have examined could be classified into two major categories: one is about effects of peer assessment on learning outcome which is focused either on cognitive or affective aspects and the other is about effects of peer assessment on the learning process. Learning outcomes differ from study to study depending on the context in which the study was conducted. The most common learning outcomes are performance and attitude. Performance is measured in terms of subject matter- related skills or general skills such as presentation skills and discussion skills. Attitude pertains to students' feeling and perception towards peer assessment interventions and is often measured along motivation and self-concepts such as self-esteem.

The effects on learning process, in most cases, are examined from the perspective of students' awareness of their own learning process. Such skills include analytical and critical skills, problem solving, intellectual flexibility, the ability to engage in reasoned discussion, self-reflection, and self-criticism (R. Johnson, 1999). Student reflection on assessment procedures is an integral part of their learning experience. Peer assessment is closely related to self-assessment in that it helps students reflect the process of carrying out the assessment task (Orsmond, 2000).

Table 2.3 shows the categories of effects of peer assessment.

Table 2.3 Effects of peer assessment

Effects on learning outcome	Performance	Content specific skills
		General skills
	Attitude	Motivation
		Self-concept (self-esteem)
Effects on learning process	Awareness of the learning process	
	Awareness of the assessment process	

In the following section, previous studies and rationale that can address the specific effects of peer assessment will be presented in two categories: Studies that investigated the effects of peer assessment on learning outcome such as performance and attitude, and those that examined the effect of peer assessment on the learning process, including metacognitive awareness.

Effects on Performance

Although many studies did not explicitly state whether they focused on the role of the assessor or assessee, most of the studies reported the potential benefits of peer assessment when the participants performed the role of the Assessor. Van Lehn, Chi, Baggett, and Murray (1995) reported that in peer assessment assessors are involved in reviewing, summarizing, clarifying, giving feedback, diagnosing misconceived knowledge, identifying missing knowledge, and considering deviations from the ideal. These cognitively demanding activities help to consolidate, reinforce, and deepen understanding of the assessor. Peer assessment gives assessors a chance to directly use the knowledge they already possess or to seek more knowledge. Therefore, assessors find a meaningful use of the subject matter for their own learning or peers' learning through peer assessment.

A variety of studies have demonstrated the benefits of peer involvement in the development of writing skills, in both k-12 and higher education settings (Brufee, 1985; Higgins, Flower, & Petraglia, 1992; Lynch & Golen, 1992), because the major activities of writing such as editing and reviewing are very similar to the process of peer assessment. For example, Topping and his colleagues (2000) studied the effect of formative peer assessment in post-graduate level writing. Their study found cognitive gains of assessors: ten subjects felt that acting as an assessor was an effective way of learning content such as transferable skills, structuring skills, and organizing skills. O'Donnell and his colleagues (1986) also showed that students could derive personal benefits from a peer editing activity. The students who played the role of editor showed improvement in their own writing.

The benefits on performance are also found in other subject areas. Tsai and his colleagues (2002) studied that the use of a networked peer assessment system to facilitate the development of inquiry-oriented activities in secondary science class. Their study revealed that students who offered detailed and constructive comments on reviewing and criticizing others' work helped them improve their own work.

In the assessing activity, peer feedback is one resource that can support students' performance. Students receive individualized feedback in peer assessment. Unlike instructor feedback, peer feedback can be given more promptly and frequently. As feedback can correct errors and seems to have potent effects on learning when a student receives it thoughtfully and positively (Bangert-Drowns, Kulik, Kulik, & Morgan, 1991), students may have various potential benefits from peer feedback.

The beneficial effects of peer feedback on performance can be applicable not only to students' learning, but also for faculty training. Kaig (2000) studied the effect of peer assessment in teaching. This study used various techniques such as classroom observation, videotaping of classes, and evaluation of course materials for peer assessment. The results of the study indicated that peer assessment help to improve instruction of the faculty members.

Although many studies generally agree that peer assessment has potential benefits on assesses' learning performance through the provision of peer feedback, many are concerned with the low validity and reliability of peer feedback.

22

Summary. Overall, studies reported that peer assessment has many potential benefits related to learning performance across subject areas. However, there are still some doubts about the potential benefits of peer assessment because of the low validity and reliability of peer assessment. For this reason, most of the studies have focused on the potential benefits of peer assessment only from the Assessor's perspective.

Effects on Attitude

Peer assessment has been found to have an impact on affective domains such as self-confidence, motivation, and sympathy for assessors (Topping, et al., 2000). Being assessors may increase students' motivation through enhanced sense of ownership and personal responsibility. Role-model theory suggests that peer assessment is likely to develop in assessors an enhanced feeling of self-esteem by requiring assessors to live up to their responsibilities. In peer assessment, assessees are put in the situation that they have to interaction with peer assessors. During the process, assessees can receive companionship form peer assessors and this may result in reduced anxiety in the assessee of assessment and improve acceptance of negative feedback (Topping, 1998).

Many studies reported that students showed positive attitude toward peer assessment (Ballantyne et al., 2002; Blom & Poole, 2004; Falchikov, 1995; Topping, 1998). Students reported they enjoyed assessing peer's work and rethinking peer's perspectives. For instance, Hunter & Russ' study on peer assessment in music performance (1996) reported that students gained confidence in expressing and articulating their views in written reports in a positive and informed manner. Smyth's study (2004) is along the same line with Hunter & Russ' study and it found that while somewhat embarrassed at first, students increased their confidence levels in critical evaluation skills.

In addition, some studies support the idea that students accept peer feedback more positively than instructor feedback (Dochy et al., 1999; Hunter & Russ, 1996; Mowl & Pain, 1995). For instance, Hunter & Russ' study (1996) on peer assessment in music performance reported that students are generally happy with the contribution of their peers towards their final result.

23

On the other hand, some studies found that students had a negative attitude. For example, Orsmond and his colleagues (1996) found that students were uncomfortable with peer assessment because they felt unqualified to assess peer's work. Similarly, Topping and his colleagues (2000) showed that students reported cognitive challenges in assessing peer's work and they disliked cognitive challenges. Furthermore, Orsmond and his colleagues (1996) found that many of students were skeptical about the value of peers' comments. McDowell (1995) also found that students were not convinced their peers would grade fairly. These negative attitudes are not toward peer assessment itself and its potential benefits of peer assessment, but centered upon the lack of confidence in their own and their peers' abilities as assessors.

Summary. Overall studies reported that students agreed on the potential benefits of peer assessment and showed positive attitude toward peer assessment as a learning method enhancing reflective thinking. However, they sometimes showed negative attitude toward peer assessment due to the lack of confidence in both their own and their peers' abilities as assessors.

Effects on Learning Process

Peer assessment offers students the opportunity to reflect about the learning process as well as the assessment process because the task of assessing others' work itself is a good strategy for learning. Students can develop insight into both the assessment and learning process during peer assessment.

Topping and his colleagues (2000) studied the effect of formative peer assessment in post-graduate level writing. The results of the study showed metacognitive gains of assessors. They found that students felt that acting as an assessor was an effective way to be more aware of the perspectives the assessor's. In addition, they had become to be conscious of their own learning process. Blom & Poole's study on peer assessment in music performance (2004) also indicated that student assessors reported their understanding on learning process deepen through observation of other's performance and self-reflection. Furthermore, the assessors reported that they understood that they were being offered another way of learning.

Benefits of the learning process can be also explained by self-regulated learning in that students (assessees) receive peer assessors' feedback as external feedback and assessees also

24

have an opportunity to reflect their own learning as internal feedback. With both the external and internal feedback, assessees adjust their strategies and/or goals and manage their learning to pursue the goals. Furthermore, assessees are likely to have the opportunity to be aware of their own learning by experiencing self-regulated learning through formative peer assessment.

Summary. Some studies agreed that peer assessment offers students the opportunity to reflect upon the learning process as well as assessment process because assessing itself is a good learning strategy. However, there has little empirical evidence to support this idea so far.

The limitations of previous studies/approaches

Several limitations of previous studies on peer assessment have been identified.

First, studies generally agree to the positive aspects of peer assessment, but most studies did not specify what kind of benefits are from which activities during peer assessment. For example, some researchers simply reported that peer assessment offers students the opportunity to reflect about their own learning. Such findings are too general to explain the specific strengths and weaknesses of peer assessment. In addition, those findings cannot give specific information on the effects of peer assessment by students' role. In other words, they cannot give the information about the effects derived from taking Assessor's role or Assessee's role.

Furthermore, in previous sections, although I tried to distinguish the effects of peer assessment by beneficial areas (effects on performance, attitude, and metacognitive awareness), previous studies did not provide detailed information for the distinction. For this reason, my proposed study classifies the effects of peer assessment based on the context of the studies, authors' intention, and so on.

Second, according to the results of the classification and reviews, the beneficial aspects to Assessors have been more frequently discussed than the beneficial aspects to Assessees. In particular, a lot of studies reported that assessing peer's work helped students improve in performance and awareness on their own learning process.

Third, on the contrary, not many studies have been conducted from Assessees' aspect. Even if there are some studies focusing on Assessees aspects, they are usually raising the issues of low quality of peer feedback. Although formative peer assessment focuses on the function of peer assessment as a learning method rather than peer-marked score or grade, low quality peer feedback is still problematic in Assessees aspects.

Fourth, there are few studies that can support the idea of the effects of peer assessment on the learning process. Although some researchers hypothesize that peer assessment may help students internalize techniques for self-regulation or metacognitive awareness by commenting on the quality of peer's work (Zimmerman, 1990; Zimmerman, Greenberg, & Weinstein, 1994), the authors don't provide strong evidences to support the ideas.

Fifth, although many studies have been reporting the effectiveness of peer assessment, most of the reporting is based on based on students' perceived value of peer assessment, not on the empirical data. For collecting data, most frequently used research methods are simple questionnaires or interview asking student's brief opinion on their own performance and attitude.

Summary. So far, not enough efforts were devoted to investigate the specific effects of peer assessment by learner's role. Further, empirical data are very rare to verify the effects of peer assessment. Therefore, based on above findings on the limitation of the previous studies, research hypotheses and rationales of my study are proposed in the next section.

Hypotheses and Rationale

The primary purpose of the study is to investigate the effects of the Assessor's role and Assessee's role on preservice teachers' metacognitive awareness, performance, and attitude in technology-related design task. The specific research questions and hypotheses are described below.

Research Question 1

What are the comparative effects of Assessor's role and Assessee's role on metacognitive awareness, performance, and attitude?

Hypothesis 1-1. The students who play either an Assessor's role or an Assessee's role will show higher metacognitive awareness than the student who do not play either of the roles. In addition, the students who play an Assessor's role will show greater metacognitive awareness than the students who play an Assessee's role.

Rationale. This study assumes that peer assessment activities are very similar to self-regulated learning processes that enhance metacognitive awareness. From this perspective, the study predicts that the students who play either an Assessor's role or an Assessee's role will show higher metacognitive awareness than the student in control group.

However, this study hypothesizes that the students who play an Assessor's role will show higher metacognitive awareness than the students who play an Assessee's role. Several studies dealing with assessors' metacognitive gains are in support of this hypothesis (Blom & Poole, 2004; Topping, et al, 2000). The studies reported that assessors showed deeper understanding on their own learning process as well as other's perspectives and they often used self-reflection. In contrast, there is no empirical evidence related to metacognitive gains from Assessee's perspective.

Hypothesis 1-2. The students who play either the Assessor's role or the Assessee's role will show higher performance than the students who do not play either of the roles. However, there will be no difference between the student who play the Assessor's role and the students who play the Assessee's role in performance for the technology-related design task.

Rationale. The hypothesis 1-2 is based on the concept of learning by design from the Assessor's role perspective. Learning by design, as discussed previously, predicts that students are likely to construct new ideas when they are actively engaged in making some type of external artifact that they can reflect upon and share with others (Papert, 1993; Resnick, et al., 1996). If Assessors are actively involved in assessing and reflection, they will improve the acquisition of provided domain knowledge and facilitate the construction of new knowledge during the assessment. Therefore, student assessors will show better performance than the students who have no experience in assessing. Many empirical studies reviewed in the previous section also support this prediction (O'Donnell, et al., 1986; Tsai, et al., 2002; Topping, et al., 2000)

This hypothesis is also based on scaffolded learning and feedback theory from Assessee's role perspective. The common aspect of the two theories is that when students get effective support (whether it is feedback or guidance) from others, the students' learning is facilitated. Assessees receive individualized peer feedback or peer guidance. As peer feedback or guidance can be given promptly and frequently unlike instructor feedback or guidance, Assessees may have a lot of advantages from peer feedback or guidance. Many empirical studies reviewed in the previous section also support this prediction (Bangert-Drowns et al., 1991; Keig, 2000).

In summary, some studies show performance improvement by playing an Assessor's role and others show it by playing an Assessee's role. In addition, the two roles have reasonable theoretical backgrounds to support their position. Therefore, this study predicts that there would be no difference between the students who play an Assessor's role and the students who play an Assessee's role in performance. However, they would outperform the students who do not have the experience of peer assessment.

Hypothesis 1-3. The students who play either an Assessor's role or an Assessee's role will show more positive attitude toward the lesson than the students who do not play either of the roles. The students who play an Assessor's role will show more positive attitude toward peer assessment than the students who play an Assessee's role.

Rationale. Role-model theory provides theoretical support for this prediction. Goodlad & Hirst (1989) stated that if students were temporarily given the role of assessor, they would be constrained by the expectations of assessees. As a result, the assessor will try to do his/her best and show improved behavior and attitude. This implies that the Assessors are likely to develop self-esteem by having to live up to their responsibilities. In addition to the responsibility, ownership is also a good motivator for assessors to have a positive attitude.

Many studies also suggested that peer assessment may promote the Assessees' sense of ownership, personal responsibility, and motivation. Therefore, this study predicts that the students who experience peer assessment - whether the students play an Assessor's role or an Assessee's role – would show more positive attitude toward the lesson. However, there are considerable numbers of studies reporting Assessees' skeptical attitude toward peer feedback due to its low quality (McDowell, 1995; Orsmond et al., 1996). For the reason, this study predicts that the students who play an Assessor's role will show significantly more positive attitude than the students who play an Assessee's role.

Research Question 2

Does the combination of playing both the Assessor's role and Assessee's role improve learner's metacognitive awareness, performance, and attitude than either of the role alone or neither role?

Hypothesis 2-1. The students who play both roles (Assessor's role + Assessee' role) will show greater metacognitive awareness than the students who play either of the role alone or the students who are in the control condition (no role).

Rationale. From this perspective of self-regulated learning, this study predicts that the students who play both the Assessor's role and Assessee's role would show higher metacognitive awareness than the students in control group.

According to Topping's review study (1998) on peer assessment, both Assessors and Assessees can have metacognitive benefits before, during, or after peer assessment. Peer assessment leads Assessors to the awareness of their own learning gaps through planning assessment, reviewing assessment task or procedure and to the awareness of other's learning gap through assessing activity. To Assessees, timely and individualized feedback is helpful to increase reflection and self-assessment. In addition, students are likely to have the synergy effects on the awareness of learning process and assessment process by playing both roles (the Assessor's role + Assessee's role). For example, if the student plays the role of Assessor, he/she will become aware of assessment process, and if he/she plays the role of Assessee, he/she will became aware of an individual learner's learning process. Therefore, the student who plays the both role are likely to have in-depth awareness of learning and assessment process by taking multiple perspectives.

Therefore, based on each beneficial aspect of the Assessor's role and the Assessee's role, and their synergy effects, this study predicts that the students taking both roles (playing both the Assessor's role and Assessee' role) would show higher metacognitive awareness than the students who take either of the role alone.

Hypothesis 2-2. The students who play both roles (Assessor's role + Assessee' role) will show greater performance than the students who play either of the role alone or the students who are in the control group.

Rationale. This prediction is along the same line with hypothesis 1-2 that there is no difference between Assessor's role and Assessee's role in performance. According to the rationale for Hypothesis 1-2, some studies and theories show beneficial aspects of the Assessor's role to performance and others show beneficial aspects of the Assessee's role to performance. Therefore, this study can expect that playing both the Assessor's role and Assessee's role would best promote performance than playing either of the roles alone or as compared to neither role (control condition).

Hypothesis 2-3. The students who play both roles (Assessor's role + Assessee' role) will indicate a more positive attitude toward the lesson and the peer assessment than the students who play either role alone or no role (control condition).

Rationale. Role-model theory provides theoretical support for this prediction. According to the role-model theory, if a student is temporarily given the role of assessor, the assessor will be constrained by the expectations of assessees (Goodlad & Hirst, 1989). Along the same vein, if a student is temporally given the role of assessee, the assessee will be constrained by the expectations of assessors. As the results, the assessor and the assessee will try to do their best and show improved behavior and attitude. Therefore, from the perspective of role-model-theory, this study predicts that the students who play both the Assessor's role and Assessee's role would show more positive attitude than the students in control group.

Although many studies have agreed that peer assessment is a good motivator for students due to students-centered design, ownership, and novelty, some studies have reported Assessees' skeptical attitude toward peers (Assessors) and peer assessment. One of the possible reasons for the skeptical attitude is based on the lack of confidence in their own and their peers' abilities as assessors (Ballantyne et al., 2002). However, this type of negative attitude is likely to be reduced by playing both roles simultaneously because playing both roles at a time is good to understand other's perspective. This idea is based on Topping and his colleague's study (2000) about formative peer assessment of academic writing. The study reported that the students who played the both roles realized the importance and difficulty of assessment, and showed empathy with others. Through deeper understanding of Assessors' role, Assessees have positive attitude by reducing negative aspects and anxiety toward peer assessors' feedback. Many studies are supporting the idea (Dochy, et al, 1999; Hunter & Russ, 1996; Mowl & Pain, 1995). Therefore, this study predicts that the students who play both the Assessor's role and Assessee's role simultaneously will show more positive attitude toward peer assessment and the lesson than the students who play either of the role alone or the students in control condition.

Research Question 3

Are there any relationships between the quality of peer feedback/Back-feedback and Assessees' metacognitive awareness, performance, and attitude?

Hypothesis 3-1. Assessees who receive high quality peer feedback will show better metacognitive awareness, performance and positive attitude than Assessees who receive low quality peer feedback.

Rationale. The prediction on the relationship between feedback quality and Assessees' performance can be hypothesized based on scaffolding and feedback theory. In scaffolded learning, the concept of ZPD supports the ideas that effective learning requires support and guidance from a somewhat advanced peer or instructor. This implies that there is minimum required quality for guidance and support for the effective use of the guidance and support. From this perspectives, some studies have been investigating the relationship between feedback quality and Assessees' performance (Daniel, 2004; Hunter & Russ, 1996; Sluijsmans, Brand-Gruwel, & vanMerrienboer, 2002).

Bloxham & West's study (2004) also supports this prediction in terms of the relationship between feedback quality and Assessees' attitude or metacognitive awareness. They found that when Assessees received high quality peer feedback based on assessment criteria, Assessees saw peer assessment as a positive experience that assisted their understanding of the assessment process. These findings replicated a number of other studies' findings (for example, Orsmond et al., 2000, 2002; Purchase, 2000; Staphani, 1998). In addition, Bloxham & West indicated that

31

receiving high quality feedback based on assessment criteria helped Assessees become aware of their achievements and better understand assessment feedback.

Hypothesis 3-2. Assessees who compose positive back-feedback (high back-feedback score) will show better metacognitive awareness, performance, and attitude than the Assessees who compose negative back-feedback (low back-feedback score).

Rationale. In general, Assessees who show better performance will receive good feedback. As they receive a good feedback, they will compose more positive back-feedback to their peer assessor. In addition, since levels of cognitive and metacognitive engagement are associated with levels of attitude (particularly, motivation) (Garcia & Pintrich, 1991), higher performers will be expected to show higher metacognitive awareness and better attitude (higher motivation) than lower performers. For this reason, it is expected that Assessees who compose positive back-feedback (high back-feedback score) will show better metacognitive awareness, performance, and attitude than the Assessees who compose negative back-feedback (low back-feedback score).

CHAPTER III

METHOD

Overview of Study Design

The purpose of this study was to examine the effect of peer assessment in a preservice teachers' technology-related design project. Specifically, it focused on the effect of student's different roles in peer assessment on student metacognitive awareness, performance and attitude: students as assesses only (receiving peer feedback) or students as assessors only (giving peer feedback), or students as both assessors and assesses.

This study primarily employed a 2 X 2 factorial design (Kirk, 1982). This design was selected because it allows the researcher to analyze the effect of each condition and make post-treatment comparisons between treatment groups and the control group. Four intact groups were assigned randomly to the three treatment groups and control group for this study. Therefore, this study was a quasi-experimental design.

The design of the study is summarized in Table 3.1. The independent variables of this study were the two different learner's roles in peer assessment: receiving peer feedback (present, absent), giving peer feedback (present, absent). According to the matrix of type of role, four different conditions result: Assessee-only role condition (only receiving peer feedback), Assessor-only role condition (only giving peer feedback), Both-roles condition (both giving and receiving feedback), and No-role condition (control group).

There were three dependent measures in this study: metacognitive awareness (change in perspective of assessment as a future teacher, self-reported regulatory skills), performance (the score of the final product), and attitude (motivation).

Table 3.1 Overview of study design

Independent variables:	Two types of learner's role in peer assessment ▪ **Assessor's role:** Assessing and giving feedback ▪ **Assessee's role:** Receiving peer feedback

Matrix of conditions:		Receiving peer feedback	
		Absent	Present
Assessing and providing peer feedback	Absent	Control group (Group A)	Assessee's role only (Group B)
	Present	Assessor's role only (Group C)	Assessee + Assessor's role (Group D)

Dependent variables:

	Specific measures
Metacognitive awareness	▪ Change in perspective of the value of peer assessment ▪ Self-reported regulatory skills for doing task
Performance	▪ Final product score
Attitude	▪ Motivation toward the Inspiration lesson and peer assessment

Participants

Participants for this study included 82 preservice teachers enrolled in the "Introduction to Educational Technology" course at a southeastern public university in spring semester, 2005.

The course is a required course for preservice teachers, and the participants were from four sections of the course taught by four different instructors. Those students who had signed the informed consent forms at the beginning of the experiment procedure participated in the study.

Demographic Information

The following is the demographic information of the 82 participants. All of the 82 students were undergraduate students. The mean age of the sample was approximately 19.57 years (SD=2.4). Among those who reported ethnicity, 74.7% are Caucasian, 6.0% are African-American, 4.8% are Hispanic, 2.4% are Asian, and 3.6% are of other ethnic groups. Among the respondents who reported gender, 81.3% of the participants were female and 16.9% were male. The majority of the participants were freshmen (41.6%) and sophomores (41.6%) with 14.3% juniors and 2.6% seniors. Regarding academic major, 35.1% are majoring in elementary education, 29% in secondary education, 10.8% in early childhood education, 6.1% in special education, and 19% in majors outside the field of education.

Determination of the Sample Size

The required sample size was estimated by using pre-determined alpha, effect size, and power. The alpha level was set to .05, the power level set to .55, and Cohen (1988)'s definition of medium effect size for 2x2 factorial design (measure of effect size for factorial design, f =.25) was set. The medium effect size was determined based on the pilot study (Kim & Ryu, 2004).

A priori power analysis was conducted to calculate the required sample size. According to the power analysis, a minimum of 18 subjects per condition is required. Therefore, at least 72 subjects were needed for this study. Since a minimum of 19 students per condition participated in this study, this study met the required sample size for 2X2 factorial design.

Task and Material

Task

Technology-related design task (concept mapping assignment). The task used for both the control and treatment conditions was an assignment to design a concept map using Inspiration (concept mapping software). All participants were asked to construct a concept map on a particular topic for instruction. The concept map must have at least ten nodes and represent concrete ideas on a particular topic for instruction. As most of participants were preservice teachers majoring in various fields, the topic for instruction was individually decided by participants so that the selected topic would be familiar to them. (See Appendix A, Sample Student Concept Map) When participants developed a concept map, the instructor encouraged them to use two types of criteria: (1) objective criteria, including required numbers of nodes, images, and web-links, and (2) subjective criteria, including clarity of structure, completeness, support, and creativity. (All of these criteria will be elaborated later in the section on "material.")

Task for assessors. Participants in two conditions (Group C & D, see Table 3.1) assessed the draft version of their peers' computer project assignment. During the assessment, the participants were instructed to use an assessment form (see Appendix B). This task took about 20 minutes to complete. However, as this study included a 10-minute training session for the peer assessment prior to the actual assessment activity, the amount of time needed for the complete activity was 30 minutes. After the assessment, assessors revised their own draft of the assignment based on their experience of assessing the peer's work.

Task for assessees. Participants in two conditions (Group B & D, see Table 3.1) received peer feedback on their own draft assignment. After receiving and reviewing the peer feedback, assessees were asked to fill out the back-feedback form (Appendix C). Back-feedback was intended to give an opportunity for the assessees to reflect on their product and peer feedback by explicitly expressing their opinion on the feedback from their peers.

After filling out the back-feedback form, assessees revised their draft assignment.

36

Material

Concept mapping software (Inspiration). A concept map consists of hierarchically arranged nodes or cells that contain concepts, items or questions and labeled links. The relationships between nodes/concepts are indicated by "linking" words and an arrow symbol to describe the direction of the relationship. An example of a concept map, developed with Inspiration, is shown below in Figure 3.1. Concept maps are particularly useful for representing networks of concepts, where links do not only connect adjacent concepts but are often linked to concepts in different sections of the concept map. The resulting web of concepts increases the number of relationships that connect new information to existing concepts thereby increasing the stability of the new information.

In addition, computer applications can provide significant support in the creation and maintenance of concept maps. Automated tools can improve visual appearance and consistency. They also facilitate the display and revision of large and / or complex maps through functions such as zooming and automatic redraw. There are many such tools available and the most popular one is probably *Inspiration*. The following example (Figure 3.1) is a concept map on African American inventors.

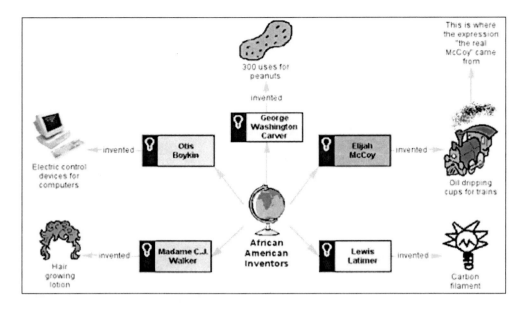

300 uses for peanuts

invented

This is where the expression "the real McCoy" came from

George Washington Carver

invented

Otis Boykin

Elijah McCoy

invented

Electric control devices for computers

Oil dripping cups for trains

African American Inventors

Madame C.J. Walker

Lewis Latimer

invented

invented

Hair growing lotion

Carbon filament

Figure 3.1 Concept map example developed with Inspiration

Peer Assessment Form. The Peer Assessment Form was developed by the researcher (See Appendix B, Peer Assessment Form). The Peer Assessment Form consisted of two parts: (1) objective assessment criteria, and (2) subjective assessment criteria. Objective assessment criteria included five objective scoring categories, including minimum 12 nodes, text in lines, different shape or images, at least one external image, and at least one web link. These objective scoring categories were identical with the requirements of the concept map assignment, which were provided to students in advance.

In contrast, subjective assessment criteria had four subjective scoring categories. These four categories were generated as a result of collaboration with instructors of the course. Through discussion, four common criteria that the instructors had used to evaluate the Inspiration assignment in prior semesters were identified: (1) clarity of structure, (2) completeness, (3) support, and (4) creativity. 'Clarity of structure' required students to construct a concept map with a good coherent and logical structure; 'completeness' required students to create a concept

38

map with all of the relevant topics and issues; 'support' required students to map their ideas with appropriate amount of supportive materials; and 'creativity' required students to generate a concept map with unique aspects. For each criterion, student assessors selected, among the three given choices, one that reflected the quality of the assignment he/she was reviewing. Then, the student assessor provided an explanation for the decision. The open-ended explanation was used to triangulate participants' response for each question. (See Appendix B-1, Sample Student Peer Assessment Form)

Back-Feedback Form. The back-feedback form was developed by the researcher (See Appendix C, Back-Feedback Form). The items in the Back-Feedback Form correspond to those of the Peer Assessment Form with the five objective scoring criteria and four subjective scoring criteria. For each criterion, assessees were asked whether they agreed with the assessor's opinion or not (i.e., "Do you agree with your peer's opinion?"). The answers were coded as 1 (Yes, I agree) or 0 (No, I disagree). Next, they were asked to describe why or why not? The Back-Feedback Form was to give assessees an opportunity to carefully review their peer feedback. (See Appendix C-1, Sample Student Back-feedback Form)

Variables

Independent Variables

The independent variables for the study included two different roles of learners in peer assessment. The learner's role was classified into two types: 1) assessor's role and 2) assessee's role. Assessor' role was to assess peer's work and provide feedback and assessee's role was to receive peer feedback. Therefore, assessing and giving feedback (assessor's role) was one independent variable, and receiving feedback (assessee's role) was another independent variable.

Each independent variable had two levels (present, absent) according to the existence of the role. Depending on the experimental condition, no role, assessor's role, assessee's role, or both roles was implemented to the participants. The participants who were in the no role condition (control group) did not experience peer assessment. The participants who were in assessor's role condition (referred to as Assessor-only) assessed peer's work and give feedback but they did not receive peer feedback on their own work. The participants who are in Assessee-only role condition did not assess peer's work but they received peer's feedback on their own work. The participants who are in "Both-roles" condition assessed peer's work and received peer feedback on their own work.

Dependent Variables

There were three dependent variables for the study: 1) metacognitive awareness, 2) performance, and 3) attitude. By employing the three different dependent variables, the researcher intended to measure and analyze the effects of different roles on those measures when learners engage in the assessment activity. Each dependent variable measure is described in the following section.

Measures

Primary Measures

Metacognitive awareness. Metacognitive awareness was measured according to two aspects: (a) change in perspective of the value of peer assessment, and (b) self-reported regulatory skills for conducting the technology-related design task.

To assess the change in perspective of the value of peer assessment, participants who engaged in peer assessment were asked whether the peer assessment that they experienced changed their perspective towards the value of peer assessment. Specifically, the participants who were in Assessor-only condition were provided the statement, "The activity of assessing your peer's work changed my perspective of the value of assessment," while the participants in Assessee-only condition were provided, "The activity of receiving peer feedback changed my perspective of the value of peer assessment." Similarly, participants in Both roles (Assessor + Assessee) condition were provided, "The activity of peer assessment changed my perspective of the value of peer assessment." A five-point Likert scale was provided as a response choices ranging from strongly disagree to strongly agree. Following that, they were asked to describe reasons for their responses (Why or why not?). Two raters (the researcher and an assistant) reviewed the answers to the open-ended question. The question about change in perspective of assessment was given only to participants in treatment conditions because participants in the control condition did not have the experience of peer assessment.

To assess participants' self-reported regulatory skills, a revised version of the Metacognitive Assessment Inventory (MAI) developed by Schraw and Dennison (1994) was used. The original MAI items were classified into eight sub-components subsumed under two broader categories: knowledge of cognition and regulation of cognition. Since this study focused on self-regulation, it used only the items on regulation of cognition with five sub-components: planning, information management, monitoring, debugging, and evaluation. To shorten the questionnaire, among the 35 original items for regulation of cognition, only 15 items (three items for each sub-component) were selected that have a large factor loading value as reported by Schraw and Dennison (1994). The original items of MAI refer to learner's regulation of cognition in a general sense, but this study changed every statement of the items based on the context. For example, an original item, "I set specific goals before I begin a task," was revised to "I set specific goals before I began revising the Inspiration assignment."

Participants were asked to answer the 15 questions based on their experience in the peer assessment. The original responses to the items are in the form of a seven-point Likert scale, but this study used five-point Likert scale (1 = strongly disagree, 2 = disagree, 3 = neutral, 4 = agree, 5 = strongly agree). Although many researchers (Bass et al, 1974; Chang, 1994; Cohen, 1983; Devlin et al, 1993) have reported that there is no best number of response options for all applications, they agree that longer scale may introduce lower reliability than shorter scale due to the lack of respondents' frames of reference. For the reason, this study used a five-point Likert scale instead of a seven-point Likert scale. The reliability of the original MAI is .90 (Schraw & Dennison, 1994), but the response reliability of the revised survey for this study was .85. (See Appendix D, Metacognitive Awareness Questionnaire)

Learning performance. Learning performance of each individual was the final assignment score assessed by two raters (the researcher and an assistant). Participants submitted their computer project assignment two times (draft submission & final submission). The first (draft) submission was completed prior to the peer assessment and the second (final) submission followed the peer assessment. The score of the draft assignment was used as a prior performance score to assess the homogeneity of prior performance level of the four groups.

In the second submission, participants revised their first draft based on the experience of peer assessment and their reflection. The score of the second (final) version of the technology-related design assignment was used as the index of learning performance. Both submitted assignments were scored by two raters. They scored participants' assignment on the basis of a scoring rubric, which was identical with the Peer Assessment Form (see Appendix E, Scoring Rubric for Performance). Accordingly, students' performance score was expressed by the objective score and subjective score. Score range for the objective assessment was a point value from 0 to 5, and that for the subjective assessment was a point value from 0 to 8.

Attitude. Participants' attitude toward peer assessment was measured with a survey designed by the researcher based on two established instruments derived from Keller's ARCS model on motivation: Course Interest Survey (CIS) (Keller, 1987) and Instructional Materials Motivational Survey (IMMS) (Keller, 1993).

The attitude survey contained 14 basic items that were the same across the four conditions and 14 additional items that were specific to participants in the three treatment conditions. The 14 basic items collected information on the participants' attitude toward the Inspiration lesson, such as whether student enjoyed the Inspiration learning. Twelve items of the 14 basic items were derived from CIS and revised. Among the original 34 items of CIS, only 12 items (three items for each sub-component: attention, relevance, confidence, and satisfaction) were selected that had showed a large factor loading value in the researcher's pilot study (Kim & Ryu, 2004). The twelve items were five-point Likert scale questions with response choices ranging from strongly disagree to strongly agree. The response reliability of the basic 12 Likert items of this study was .84. The two remaining items were open-ended questions to collect information on student likes and dislikes as to the Inspiration lesson.

Fourteen additional items were added to the 14 basic items for participants in treatment conditions to gather information specific to each of the three treatment conditions. The 14 additional items collected information on the participants' attitude toward the peer assessment, such as whether student enjoyed the peer assessment activity. Twelve items of the 14 additional items were derived from IMMS and revised. Among the original 36 items of IMMS, only 12 items (three items for each sub-component: attention, relevance, confidence, and satisfaction) were selected that had showed a large factor loading value in the researcher's pilot study (Kim & Ryu, 2004). The twelve items were five-point Likert scale questions. The response reliability of the additional 12 Likert items of this study was .82. The two remaining items were open-ended questions dealing with student likes and dislikes regarding the peer assessment. (See Appendix F, Attitude Survey)

Additional Measures

Participants' demographic information. Prior to the treatment, the researcher gave the participants a short survey for demographic information including age, gender, ethnicity, grade level, and major field of study (For the questionnaire, see Appendix G). These questions provided the researcher with information on the distribution of participants across the conditions. Approximately 5 minutes were used for the survey.

Participants' prior metacognitive awareness level. Prior to the treatment, five general metacognitive awareness questions, derived from MAI (Metacognitive Awareness Inventory), were provided across four conditions to assess the homogeneity of prior metacognitive awareness level of the four groups. (See Appendix H) Approximately 5 minutes were used for the questions.

Participants' prior attitude level. Prior to the treatment, four attitude questions in terms of motivation, derived from CIS (Course Interest Survey), were provided across four conditions to assess the homogeneity of prior attitude level (specifically, prior motivation level toward the

43

course) of the four groups. (See Appendix I) Approximately 5 minutes were used for the questions.

Assessors' feedback. Two raters evaluated the peer assessment form filled out by assessors. For the evaluation, the two raters used the Evaluation Form for Peer Assessment Form (see Appendix B-2) to assess the quality of peer assessment. The assessor's feedback was assigned a point value from zero to ten by the raters and used for further analyses, including the correlation between participants' learning performance and the quality of peer feedback. The inter-rater reliability of the two raters was .85.

Assessees' back-feedback. Two raters evaluated the responses from the back-feedback form filled out by assessees. For the evaluation, the two raters also used another evaluation form (see Appendix C-2) to assess the quality of Assessees' back-feedback.

For the five questions that asked if you agree with your peer's opinion or not, a positive answer (agree) was coded as "1" and negative answer (disagree) was coded as "0." For the five open-ended questions ("why or why not?" questions) that asked the reasons, two raters assigned a point value from zero to two for each criterion. If an assessee provided reasonable rationale for his/her opinion, "2 point" was assigned. If an assessee provided rationale for his/her opinion but not clear, "1 point" was assigned. For missed written feedback, "0 point" was assigned. The inter-rater reliability of the two raters was .91. The back-feedback score of Assessees was also used for further analyses, including the correlation between Assessees' attitude and back-feedback score.

Table 3.2 is a summary of measures, measuring tools, and type of data that were employed in this study.

Table 3.2 Summary of measures

Prior to Study		
Measures	Measuring tools	Type of data
• Demographic information	▪ Demographic survey	○ Open-ended question or multiple choice
• Prior metacognitive awareness	▪ Prior metacognitive awareness survey	○ Five-item five point Likert scale questions
• Prior performance	▪ Draft assignment (concept map)	○ Average score rated by two raters
• Prior attitude	▪ Prior attitude survey	○ Five-item five point Likert-scale questions
Primary Dependent Measures		
Measures	Measuring tools	Type of data
Metacognitive awareness		
• Change in perspective of the value of peer assessment	▪ Metacognitive Awareness Questionnaire	○ One-item five point Likert-scale question ○ One "Why or Why not" open-ended question
• Self-reported regulatory skills for doing task	▪ Metacognitive Awareness Questionnaire	○ 15 five point Likert-scale items with five sub-components
Performance		
• Final product score	▪ Scoring rubric for Inspiration assignment	○ Average score rated by two raters
Attitude		
• Motivation toward peer assessment and the Inspiration lesson	▪ Learner Attitude Survey	○ 24 (treatment group) or 12 (control group) five-point Likert-scale items with four sub-components ○ Four (treatment group) or two-item (control group) open-ended questions
Further Assessment		
Measures	Measuring tools	Type of data
• The quality of peer feedback	▪ Evaluation Form for Peer Assessment Form	○ Average score rated by two raters

• The quality of back-feedback	▪ Evaluation Form for Back-feedback Form	○ Average score rated by two raters
		  ▪ Agree/Disagree questions score
		  ▪ Open-ended question score

45

Procedure

Stage 1. Preparation

This study used four intact groups from the course of "Introduction to Educational Technology" in spring semester, 2005. Each group consisted of approximately 22 preservice teachers. The four groups were randomly assigned to either control group or treatment groups.

The participants were given informed consent forms at the beginning of the course (see appendix J). For those who agreed to participate in the study, they were asked to respond to a short survey for demographic information including age, gender, ethnicity, education level, and major field of study. Then, the participants were provided short questionnaires to measure prior metacognitive awareness and prior attitude.

Stage 2. Submitting Draft Assignment

Upon completion of their assignment, the students uploaded their first draft of the technology-related design assignment on the web to submit it to their instructor. Two raters (the researcher and an assistant) scored students' drafts as a prior performance score to assess homogeneity among the groups. If the groups were not homogeneous, the score of the draft assignment would be used as a covariate for assessing participants' performance. After collecting students' drafts, the researcher removed students' name from the drafts to guarantee the anonymity of peer assessment.

Right before the next class time, the researcher randomly assigned the anonymous assessees' draft to a peer assessor in Group C (Assessor-only role) and Group D (Both-roles: assessor's role + assessee's role) through web (specifically, a bulletin board of Blackbard was used) for assessment activity of assessors.

Stage 3. Conducting Peer Assessment

Before conducting peer assessment, Group C (Assessor-only role) and Group D (Both-roles: assessor's role + assessee's role) were trained how to assess peer's work. Overall, the purpose of the 10-minute training session was to acquaint the participants who play the role of the Assessor with the notion of assessment criteria and how to fill out the Peer Assessment Form. Instructors trained the participants by letting them assess an example concept map in the training material (see Appendix B-3, Training material for peer assessment).

Immediately after the training session, the assessors in Group C (Assessor's role) and Group D (Assessor's role +Assessee's role) were asked to download the assigned peer's draft from Blackboard and assess it in 20 minutes using the Peer Assessment Form. After finishing the assessment, the assessors uploaded Peer Assessment Form on the web to submit it to their instructor.

Stage 4. Providing Feedback to Assessee

After collecting the Peer Assessment Forms from Assessors (Group C & D), the instructor distributed them to Assessees (Group B & D) with their original draft assignment through web. At the same time, all other students in the four different conditions received their original draft assignment.

Then, Assessees (Group B & D) were asked to provide their opinion on the peer feedback in Back-Feedback Form. Upon completion, Assessees also submitted the Back-Feedback form to instructor through web. The back-feedback was not delivered to peer Assessors because back-feedback activity was used only for Assessee's reflection.

Stage 5. Revising the Draft

After finishing these peer assessment activities, students were asked to revise their draft and resubmit it to their instructor through web. The instructor encouraged students in the treatment groups to revise their draft based on the peer assessment experience and their own reflection. The students in the control group were asked to revise their draft on the basis of their reflections. Specifically, the participants in the treatment groups were provided this instruction: "Revise your draft concept mapping assignment based on your peer assessment experience. Remember the several assessment criteria that you used in peer assessment activity. You have to consider required numbers of nodes, images, and web links, as well as clarity of structure, completeness, support, and creativity." In contrast, the participants in the control group were provided this instruction: "Revised your draft concept mapping assignment based on your reflection. You have to consider required numbers of nodes, images, and web links, as well as clarity of structure, completeness, support, and creativity."

The revised concept mapping assignment was the final product and it served as a post-test. Two raters (the researcher and an assistant) scored the participant's final version of assignment. The score was used as the participant's learning performance. The scoring of the final version of the assignment was done by blind review with students' name and class removed from the documents so as to reduce raters' subjective judgments on the different groups.

Stage 6. Conducting Post Survey

After finishing submitting final assignment, the researcher presented the participants two surveys: metacognitive awareness questionnaire and attitude survey. Each survey took about 15 minutes to complete.

Assignment of groups to treatment groups

↓

Demographic Information Survey

Prior metacognitive awareness & Prior attitude survey

↓

Treatments

Group A (Control)	Group B (Assessee-only) (Receiving feedback)	Group C (Assessor-only) (Giving feedback)	Group D (Assessors + Assessees) (Receiving & giving peer feedback)
▪ Instruction on Inspiration	▪ Instruction on Inspiration	▪ Instruction on Inspiration	▪ Instruction on Inspiration
▪ Submitting first draft	▪ Submitting first draft	▪ Submitting first draft	▪ Submitting first draft
		▪ Training on doing assessment	▪ Training on doing assessment
		▪ Assign peer's draft to Assessors	▪ Assign peer's draft to Assessors
		▪ **Assessing peer's draft** and submit	▪ **Assessing peer's draft** and submit
	▪ Delivering peer feedback to Assessees		▪ Delivering peer feedback to Assessees
	▪ **Receiving peer feedback**		▪ **Receiving peer feedback**
	▪ **Filling out back-feedback form** and submit		▪ **Filling out back-feedback form** and submit
▪ Prompting students to reflect	▪ Prompting students to reflect	▪ Prompting students to reflect	▪ Prompting students to reflect
▪ Revising draft	▪ Revising draft	▪ Revising draft	▪ Revising draft
▪ Submitting final product	▪ Submitting final product	▪ Submitting final product	▪ Submitting final product

Final Product (performance)

↓

Metacognitive Awareness Survey

↓

Attitude Survey

Figure 3.2 Summary of experimental Procedure

(* Note: Shaded cell shows instructors and researcher's activities.)

Data Analyses

Metacognitive Awareness

The metacognitive awareness data was analyzed according to two groups of dependent measures: (a) change in perspective of the value of peer assessment, and (b) self-reported regulatory skills. As a dependent measure, change in perspective of the value of peer assessment, was only for treatment groups, one-item five-point Likert scale question that indicated the change in perspective of the value of peer assessment was assessed using one-way analysis of variance (ANOVA) with three treatment groups. For the open-ended question on the change in perspective of the value of peer assessment (i.e., "Why or Why not?"), two raters reviewed participants' response using the following five coding categories: (1) peer assessment was a new or different assessment method; (2) peer assessment enhanced understanding of my own learning; (3) peer assessment helped me have multiple perspectives; (4) peer assessment was good, but superficial; and (5) other. Each participant response could have multiple codes. The coding for the open-ended question was done by blind review with students' name and class removed from the documents so as to reduce raters' subjective judgments on the different groups.

Self-regulatory skills were assessed using two-factor multivariate analyses of variance (MANOVA) across all four conditions to examine the main effect and interaction effect of assessor's role and assessee's role. For this MANOVA, the mean score of five sub-constructs of self-regulatory skills was used. Additionally, a one-factor MANOVA by condition was conducted to investigate significant differences across the four conditions.

Performance

Two-factor MANOVA was used to determine the effect of two independent variables (Assessor's role, Assessee's role) on the two types of performance scores (objective score and subjective score). Additionally, a one-factor MANOVA by condition was conducted to investigate significant difference among the four conditions.

50

Attitude

As the 12 basic Likert-scale items that were the same across the four conditions were derived from Keller's CIS with four sub-constructs of motivation (ARCS: attention, relevance, confidence, and satisfaction), two-factor (Assessor's role & Assessee's role) multivariate analysis of variance (MANOVA) was employed to reveal main effect and interaction effect of the two factors on the four sub-motivational constructs.

Mean scores for additional 12 Likert-scale items for three treatment groups were analyzed separately. For the analysis of the additional 12 items, a one-factor MANOVA (by condition: Assessor-only role, Assessee-only role, and Both-roles) was conducted because the additional 12 items were derived from Keller's IMMS with four sub-constructs of motivation.

Analysis of qualitative data from the open-ended questions was analyzed separately. Coding categories were constructed based on the emerging themes from the participants' answers. Two raters reviewed for the coding of the open-ended questions by blind review with students' name and class removed from the documents so as to reduce raters' subjective judgments on the different groups

Additional Data Analyses

The quality of peer feedback and the quality of back-feedback were used to conduct further analysis. These additional data was used to examine the relationship between peer feedback quality or back-feedback quality and other dependent measures (Assessee's metacognitive awareness, performance, and attitude) through correlational analysis.

Table 3.3 provides a summary of research question, measures for the research question, measures, question/data type, and methods for data analysis method.

Table 3.3 Data analyses

Primary data analyses			
Research question	Measures	Question/Data type	Data analysis method
Metacognitive awareness			
Research question 1 ■ What are the comparative effects of the Assessor's role and Assessee's role on metacognitive awareness, performance, and attitude?	■ Change in perspective of the value of peer assessment *(only for treatment groups)*	One five-point Likert scale item (score range 1~5) One "Why or Why not" question (open-ended)	→ One-way ANOVA with three treatment groups → Qualitative data analysis with five pre-decided coding categories
	■ Self-reported regulatory skills for doing task	15 five-point Likert scale items with five sub-constructs (average score range 1~5)	→ 2X2 MAVOVA for the mean of each sub-construct → One-factor MANOVA by condition with four groups
Research question 2 ■ Does playing both roles improve learner metacognitive awareness, performance, and attitude than either of the role alone?	**Performance**		
	■ Final assignment score	Average score rated by two raters (Average score 0~13)	→ 2x2 MANOVA → One-factor MANOVA by condition
	Attitude		

52

Table 3.3 Continued

Research question	Measures	Question/Data type	Data analysis method
	• Motivation toward peer assessment and the Inspiration lesson	• 12 basic five-point Likert items (for all conditions) about four sub-constructs (ARCS) of motivation	For 12 basic items: 2X2 MANOVA for the mean of four sub-constructs. One factor MANOVA by condition
		• 12 additional Likert items (for three treatment conditions) about four sub-constructs (ARCS) of motivation	For 12 additional items: One-factor MANOVA with three treatment groups for the mean of each sub-construct
		Four (for the treatment group) or two (for the control group) open-ended questions	Qualitative data analysis with emerging coding categories

Additional data analyses

Research question	Measures	Question/Data type	Data analysis method
Research question 3 • Is there a relationship between the quality of peer assessment and Assessees' metacognitive awareness, performance, and attitude?	• The quality of peer feedback	Average score rated by two raters (score range 0~10)	Correlation study. For the relationship between the quality of peer feedback and Assessee's metacognitive awareness, performance, & attitude

Table 3.3 Continued

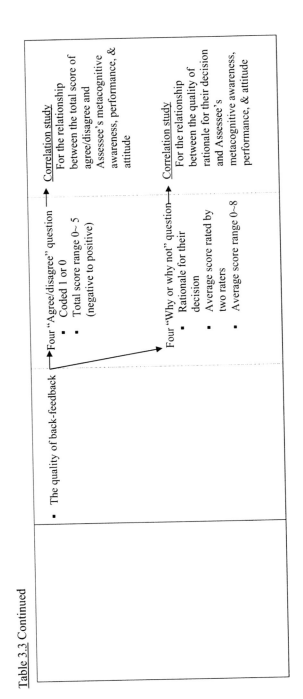

- The quality of back-feedback

Four "Agree/disagree" question
- Coded 1 or 0
- Total score range 0~5 (negative to positive)

Correlation study
For the relationship between the total score of agree/disagree and Assessee's metacognitive awareness, performance, & attitude

Four "Why or why not" question
- Rationale for their decision
- Average score rated by two raters
- Average score range 0~8

Correlation study
For the relationship between the quality of rationale for their decision and Assessee's metacognitive awareness, performance, & attitude

CHAPTER IV
RESULTS

This study was an examination of the effects of assessor's role and assessee's role on metacognitive awareness, performance, and attitude. This chapter reports the results from an analysis of data collected during this study. For the purpose of presenting the results, this chapter is divided into four sections.

In the first section, the results of preliminary data analyses prior to the statistical analysis of the dependent measures are reported. Several tests were conducted to establish equivalency of treatment groups, and to determine whether the assumptions for parametric statistics were upheld. An alpha level of .05 was used for all statistical tests.

In the second section, the results of primary data analyses of the dependent variables are reported. Hypotheses 1 and 2 regarding main effects and interaction effects of the Assessor's role and the Assessee's role were tested based on dependent variables and the results are reported.

In the third section, additional data analyses on the relationship between the quality of peer assessment and dependent variables are summarized. This data provided information for richer analyses and interpretations of the research findings. In addition, hypotheses 3, regarding the relationship between the quality of peer assessment and dependent variables, was tested and the results are reported.

In the last section, all results are summarized.

Preliminary Data Analyses

In this section, the equivalence of treatment groups was tested. Then, a missing value analysis, a case analysis, and a detection of violations for the main dependent variables were conducted as the foundation for the primary data analyses.

Information for Group Equivalence

Since this study employed quasi-experimental design, the equivalence across the groups had to be investigated. To investigate the equivalence of treatment groups, three variables - student's prior metacognitive awareness, prior performance, and prior attitude – were analyzed.

Prior metacognitive awareness. One-way ANOVA was conducted to examine possible differences in students' prior metacognitive awareness level. The results were not significant [$F(3,78)=2.411$, MSE=1.169, $p>.05$]. It indicated that prior metacognitive awareness level was not significantly different across treatment groups.

Prior performance. One-way ANOVA was conducted to examine possible differences in students' prior performance level, and it was not significant [$F(3,78)=.900$, MSE=4.244, $p>.05$]. It indicated that prior performance level was not significantly different across treatment groups.

Prior attitude. One-way ANOVA was conducted to examine possible differences in students' prior attitude level. The results were not significant [$F(3,78)=1.679$, MSE=.347, $p>.05$]. It indicated that prior attitude was not significantly different across treatment groups.

Conducting a Missing Data Analysis

The data for prior level of metacognitive awareness, performance, and attitude and the data for the three main dependent variables (metacognitive awareness, performance, and attitude) were measured. Several missing values were found in the variables because of students' absence in the first week or the second week of this study. (This experiment was conducted over two weeks in regular class time) Expectation-Maximization (EM) method in missing value analysis was used to fill in missing values. Expectation-Maximization (EM) method is for the estimation of mean values and covariance matrices from incomplete datasets, and the imputation of missing values in incomplete datasets (Schneider, 2001). The resulting sample sizes were: Control group $n = 19$, Assessor + Assessee's role group $n = 22$, Assessor's role group $n = 21$, and Assessee's role group $n = 20$.

Conducting a Case Analysis

As the major statistical method for data analyses of this study is MANOVA, a case analysis was also conducted to detect multivariate outliers. Multivariate outliers as cases with extreme values with respect to multiple variables were detected by Mahalanobis distance. An initial screening of the data suggested that there were two outliers, one in the Control group and one in the Assessee's role group. A sensitivity analysis considering the change in sample statistics due to dropping these two outliers indicated that they did not exert any influence on the results, so the outliers were retained.

Tests for the Assumptions for Initially Planned Tests

As the major statistical method for data analyses of this study is MANOVA, each of the following three assumptions that should be satisfied for the MANOVA test were examined.

Assumption 1: Independence. A logical analysis of sampling and study circumstances were conducted to identify possible sources of lack of independence. As this study used non-repeated measures and random sampling for treatment groups, the assumption of independence was satisfied.

Assumption 2: Multivariate normality. MANOVA test requires that all the dependent variables are multivariate normal (Stevens, 1996). To detect the violations of this assumption,

57

visual inspection of graphical representations of the data and an examination of formal statistical analyses were conducted for each dependent variable and group. For the formal statistical analyses, the Shapiro-Wilk test that is applicable to the normality test for small sample sizes was used (see Table 4.1, Table 4.2, and Table 4.3). Results indicated that a few dependent measures of each group were not normally distributed. However, the degree of violation was trivial and type I error for MANOVA is robust to moderate violations of this assumption.

Table 4.1 Shapiro-Wilk normality tests for metacognitive awareness

Five constructs of metacognitive awareness	Condition	Shapiro-Wilk statistic	df	Sig.
Planning	Control group	.967	19	.658
	Assessor + Assessee	.901*	22	.032
	Assessor group	.941	21	.222
	Assessee group	.920	20	.131
Information management	Control group	.876*	19	.018
	Assessor + Assessee	.936	22	.162
	Assessor group	.942	21	.241
	Assessee group	.927	20	.110
Monitoring	Control group	.919	19	.056
	Assessor + Assessee	.931	22	.126
	Assessor group	.968	21	.691
	Assessee group	.927	20	.136
Debugging	Control group	.921	19	.102
	Assessor + Assessee	.952	22	.366
	Assessor group	.914	21	.065
	Assessee group	.899*	20	.040
Evaluation	Control group	.946	19	.283
	Assessor + Assessee	.918	22	.068
	Assessor group	.914	21	.066
	Assessee group	.901*	20	.043

Table 4.2 Shapiro-Wilk normality tests for performance

Two criteria of performance	Condition	Shapiro-Wilk statistic	df	Sig.
Objective score	Control group	.920	19	.101
	Assessor + Assessee	.929	22	.122
	Assessor group	.849*	21	.004
	Assessee group	.944	20	.228
Subjective score	Control group	.922	19	.106
	Assessor + Assessee	.919	22	.072
	Assessor group	.929	21	.133
	Assessee group	.901*	20	.044

Table 4.3 Shapiro-Wilk normality tests for attitude

Four constructs of attitude	Condition	Shapiro-Wilk statistic	df	Sig.
Attention	Control group	.949	19	.378
	Assessor + Assessee	.918	22	.071
	Assessor group	.937	21	.193
	Assessee group	.922	20	.108
Relevance	Control group	.940	19	.370
	Assessor + Assessee	.947	22	.277
	Assessor group	.960	21	.688
	Assessee group	.913	20	.073
Competence	Control group	.918	19	.103
	Assessor + Assessee	.910*	22	.047
	Assessor group	.919	21	.082
	Assessee group	.934	20	.180
Satisfaction	Control group	.850*	19	.007
	Assessor + Assessee	.927	22	.108
	Assessor group	.947	21	.292
	Assessee group	.932	20	.171

Assumption 3: Constant variance-covariance matrix assumption. Box's test was used to test the null hypothesis that the observed covariance matrices of the dependent variables were

equal across groups (see Table 4.4, Table 4.5, and Table 4.6). As the Box's tests were not significant, there was no evidence of a violation of the constant covariance matrix assumption.

Table 4.4 Box's test of equality of covariance matrices for metacognitive awareness

Box's M	56.130
F	1.099
df1	45
df2	14238.114
Sig.	.301

Table 4.5 Box's test of equality of covariance matrices for performance

Box's M	12.779
F	1.354
df1	9
df2	66307.450
Sig.	.203

Table 4.6 Box's test of equality of covariance matrices for attitude

Box's M	46.333
F	1.397
df1	30
df2	15799.055
Sig.	.073

For the specific investigation on any variance or correlation differences across the groups, Levene's test was conducted. Levene's test of the assumption of homogeneity of variance for each of the dependent variables resulted in fail to reject decisions for all variables, a result consistent with the assumption that the variances were equal over the groups (see Table 4.7, Table 4.8, and Table 4.9). The consistency between these results and the box's test results supported that there is no evidence of a violation of constant variance-covariance matrix.

Table 4.7 Levene's test of equality of error variances for metacognitive awareness

	F	df1	df2	Sig.
Planning	.234	3	78	.872
Information management	1.818	3	78	.151
Monitoring	.957	3	78	.417
Debugging	1.376	3	78	.256
Evaluation	.073	3	78	.974

Table 4.8 Levene's test of equality of error variances for performance

	F	df1	df2	Sig.
Objective score	1.338	3	78	.268
Subjective score	1.843	3	78	.146

Table 4.9 Levene's test of equality of error variances for attitude

	F	df1	df2	Sig.
Attention	1.826	3	78	.149
Relevance	.439	3	78	.726
Competence	2.061	3	78	.112
Satisfaction	1.771	3	78	.160

Examination of Specific Dependent Variables for Hypotheses 1 & 2

This section reports descriptive data for the dependent variables and results from the statistical tests. In the following sub-sections, results are described for metacognitive awareness (quantitative and qualitative), performance (quantitative), and attitude (quantitative and qualitative). In particular, results from the testing of hypotheses 1 (the comparative effects of the Assessor's role and the Assessee's role) and hypotheses 2 (the effects of the Assessor+Assessee role) are reported.

61

Descriptive Data

The descriptive statistics for all dependent variables are presented in Table 4.10. This table is organized according to the presence and absence of the Assessor's role and Assessee's role (i.e., main effect) and, also according to the four participant conditions (No-role, Assessor-only role, Assessee-only role, and Both-roles). To test hypotheses 1 (comparative effects of Assessor's role and Assessee's role), two-factor analyses by main effects are conducted. On the other hand, to test hypotheses 2 (differences among conditions), one-factor analyses by condition are conducted.

Table 4.10 Descriptive statistics for the dependent variables

Dependent Variable	Measures		By Main Effects				By Condition			
			Assessor's role		Assessee's role		No-role	Assessor-only role	Assessee-only role	Both-roles
			absent (n=39)	present (n=43)	absent (n=40)	present (n=42)	(n=19)	(n=22)	(n=21)	(n=20)
Metacognitive Awareness	* Change in perspective [a]	M	N/A	N/A	N/A	N/A	N/A	3.68	3.45	3.10
		SD						.89	.51	.87
	Self-reported regulatory skills [b]									
	1. planning	M	3.44	3.61	3.31	3.75	3.14	3.46	3.73	3.76
		SD	.60	.53	.51	.53	.48	.51	.55	.53
	2. Information management	M	3.18	3.37	3.20	3.36	3.11	3.29	3.25	3.45
		SD	.52	.61	.45	.68	.30	.54	.67	.68
	3. Monitoring	M	3.71	3.69	3.62	3.78	3.61	3.62	3.80	3.76
		SD	.53	.60	.47	.61	.49	.47	.57	.65
	4. Debugging	M	3.89	4.01	3.91	3.99	3.74	4.06	4.03	3.95
		SD	.73	.52	.65	.61	.70	.57	.75	.46
	5. Evaluation	M	3.38	3.63	3.33	3.67	3.16	3.49	3.58	3.76
		SD	.55	.58	.55	.56	.50	.55	.53	.58
Performance	Assignment score									
	1. Objective score	M	3.64	3.79	3.53	3.90	3.05	3.95	4.20	3.64
		SD	.93	.91	.93	.88	.85	.80	.62	1.00
	2. Subjective score [d]	M	5.31	5.26	5.43	5.14	5.21	5.62	5.40	4.91
		SD	1.42	1.42	1.52	1.30	1.69	1.36	1.14	1.41
Attitude	Toward the lesson [e]									
	1. Attention	M	3.47	3.63	3.51	3.60	3.54	3.48	3.40	3.77
		SD	.60	.58	.45	.70	.42	.48	.73	.64
	2. Relevance	M	3.73	3.91	3.61	4.03	3.58	3.63	3.87	4.18
		SD	.67	.62	.62	.61	.63	.63	.70	.48
	3. Competence	M	3.79	3.95	3.87	3.87	3.96	3.79	3.63	4.09
		SD	.58	.60	.54	.64	.43	.62	.66	.55
	4. Satisfaction	M	3.71	3.81	3.60	3.92	3.53	3.67	3.88	3.95
		SD	.56	.65	.55	.63	.43	.63	.62	.64
	* Toward peer assessment [f]									
	1. Attention	M	N/A	N/A	N/A	N/A	N/A	3.12	3.65	3.42
		SD						.70	.66	.69
	2. Relevance	M	N/A	N/A	N/A	N/A	N/A	3.33	3.48	3.51
		SD						.69	.63	.61
	3. Competence	M	N/A	N/A	N/A	N/A	N/A	3.46	3.08	3.98
		SD						.63	.98	.94
	4. Satisfaction	M	N/A	N/A	N/A	N/A	N/A	3.11	3.27	3.30
		SD						.61	.80	.82

Notes:

a: Possible range for change in perspective (1-5)
b: Possible range for each measure of self-reported regulatory skills (1-5)
c: Possible range for object score (0-5)
d: Possible range for subject score (0-8)
e: Possible range for each measure of attitude toward the lesson (1-5)
f: Possible range for each measure of attitude toward peer assessment (1-5)

* Measure only for three treatment conditions.

Metacognitive Awareness

Metacognitive awareness was measured according to two aspects: (1) change in perspective of the value of peer assessment after experiencing peer assessment and (2) self-reported regulatory skills for conducting the technology-related design task.

Change in perspective of the value of peer assessment. One-item Likert scale question for change perspective of the value of peer assessment was analyzed through one-way ANOVA, because the question was given only to three treatment groups after experiencing peer assessment. The one-way ANOVA indicated that $F(2,62)=3.063$, MSE=1.842, $p=.054$. The ANOVA test revealed that there was no significant difference in change perspective of the value of peer assessment after playing different role in peer assessment (whether it is assessor' role, assessee's role or both roles).

Of the 63 participants who responded to the question for change of perspective, 52 provided reasons by open-ended answers. Two raters categorized their qualitative reasons based on pre-categorized categories. Cohen's Kappa of inter-rater agreement for nominal scale is .81. According to the results of qualitative analyses, many students cited peer assessment activity helped to enhance understanding of their own learning (e.g., "Assessing peer's work made me think more in-depth about the assignment") whether they played the role of assessor, assessee, or both. On the contrary, many other students cited that the peer assessment activity was good, but it was superficial (e.g., "Peer assessment is helpful, but I didn't receive enough feedback...I didn't change my perspective of the value of peer assessment"). All the three conditions showed a similar frequency pattern for each of the coding categories. Accordingly, chi-square analyses revealed no significant differences among the frequencies represented by these categories.

Table 4.11 Percentages of categorical responses for change in perspective by conditions

	Condition		
Category of response	Assessor-only role (n=16)	Assessee-only role (n=16)	Both-roles (n=20)
Peer assessment was new or different assessment method	6%	6%	10%
Peer assessment enhanced understanding of my own learning	36%	42%	20%
Peer assessment helped me have multiple perspectives	12%	12%	15%
Peer assessment was good, but superficial	36%	30%	45%
Others	10%	10%	10%

Self-reported regulatory skills. Fifteen five-point Likert items were used to measure self-reported regulatory skills with five sub-constructs. To test hypothesis 1-1 (comparative effects of Assessor's role and Assessee's role on metacognitive awareness), the fifteen items for self-reported regulatory skills were analyzed through a two-factor MANOVA, with five sub-constructs (planning, information management, monitoring, debugging, and evaluation) as the dependent measures, and with the assessor's role (present, absent) and the assessee's role (present, absent) as the two between-subject factors. The two factor MANOVA indicated that there was an overall effect of the assessee's role on self-reported regulatory skills, Wilks Lambda=.804, $F(5,74)=3.599$, $p<.05$, $\eta^2=.196$.

Follow-up ANOVA analysis indicated that significant differences occurred in two dependent measures: planning and evaluation. Univariate results revealed a main effect for the assessee's role on planning and evaluation, indicating that the students who played an assessee role might plan and evaluate more when working on their own assignment than the students who did not play an assessee role (see Table 4.12)

Table 4.12 Main effects for Assessee's role on planning and evaluation.

Dependent measure	Type III Sum of Squares	df	MS	F	P	η^2
Planning	4.050	1	4.050	15.190	.000	.163
Evaluation	2.439	1	2.439	8.230	.005	.095

To test hypothesis 2-1 (difference among conditions), another quantitative analysis (one-factor MANOVA by condition) was conducted. According to the multiple comparisons between each two conditions, the Assessee-only role condition and Both-roles condition showed significantly higher scores than No-role condition in planning. In evaluation, only the Both-roles condition showed significantly higher score than the No-role condition (see Table 4.13).

Table 4.13 Group comparisons

Dependent measure	Group		Mean difference (I-J)	SD	P	95% CI	
	(I)	(J)				Lower	Upper
Planning	No-role	Assessee-only role	-.6172	.1617	.002	-1.0418	-.1927
		Both-roles	-.5930	.1654	.003	-1.0272	-.1587
Evaluation	No-role	Both-roles	-.5997	.1705	.004	-1.0473	-.1520

Performance

Students' performance was measured by the score of their final Inspiration assignment. The score of final assignment consisted of two components: (1) objective score and (2) subjective score. Therefore, to test hypothesis 1-2 (comparative effects of Assessor's role and Assessee's role on performance), performance was analyzed through the two-factor MONOVA design, with objective score and subjective score as the dependent measures.

The two-factor MANOVA on performance scores yielded an overall effect of the assessee's role and an interaction effect on performance. The main effect of assessee's role on performance was Wilks Lambda=.898, $F(2,77)$=4.459, $p<.05$, η^2=.104. Follow-up ANOVA indicated that significant differences occurred in the objective score of performance. The interaction effect on performance was Wilks Lambda=.831, $F(2,77)$=7.812, $p<.05$, η^2=.169. ANOVA also indicated that significant differences occurred in the objective score of performance.

Univariate results revealed a main effect for the assessee's role on the objective score. The results indicated that the students who played an assessee role received a higher object performance score than the students who did not play an assessee role, $F(1,78)$=5.083, $p<.05$, η^2 =.061. Univariate results also revealed an interaction effect for the assessor's role and assessee's role on the objective score of performance. The results indicated that the students who played only one role (whether it is the assessor's role or the assessee's role) receive higher objective score of performance than the student who played no role or both roles, $F(1,78)$=15.750, $p<.05$, η^2 =.168 (see Figure 4.1)

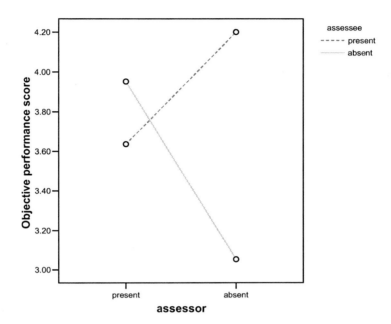

Figure 4.1 Interaction effects of the Assessor's role and the Assessee's role on objective score of performance

To test hypothesis 2-2 (differences among the conditions), another quantitative analysis (one-factor MANOVA by condition) was conducted. According to multiple comparisons between each of the two conditions, the Assessor-only role condition and Assessee-only role condition showed significantly higher score than No-role condition in objective score (see Table 4.14).

Table 4.14 Group comparisons

Dependent measure	Group		Mean difference (I-J)	SD	P	95% CI	
	(I)	(J)				Lower	Upper
Objective score	No-role	Assessor-only role	-.8998	.2639	.006	-1.5926	-.2069
		Assessee-only role	-.1.1474	.2670	.000	-1.8484	-.4464

Attitude

Students' attitude was measured by two aspects: (1) post-intervention motivation toward the Inspiration lesson, and (2) post-intervention motivation toward the peer assessment activities. While motivation toward the lesson was measure across all the conditions, motivation toward the peer assessment activities was measure only in three treatment conditions because control condition didn't have peer assessment activities. Each motivation was measured by four sub-dependent measures: attention, relevance, competence, and satisfaction.

Motivation toward the Inspiration lesson. To test hopothesis 1-3 (comparative effects of Assessor's role and Assessee's role on motivation toward the lesson), a two-factor MANOVA was conducted, with four sub-measures including attention, relevance, competence, and satisfaction. The two factor MANOVA indicated that there was an overall effect of an interaction between assessor's role and ssessee's role on motivation toward the Inspiration lesson, Wilks Lambda=.870, $F_{(4,75)}=2.808$, $p<.05$, $\eta^2 =.130$. ANOVA indicated that significant differences occurred in confidence.

Univariate results revealed an interaction effect of Assessor's role and Assessee's role on confidence toward the lesson. The results indicated that the students who played both roles or did not play any of the roles showed more confidence toward the lesson than the students who played only one of the roles (whether it is assessor's role or assessee's role), $F_{(1,78)}=6.197$, $p<.05$, $\eta^2 =.074$ (see Figure 4.2).

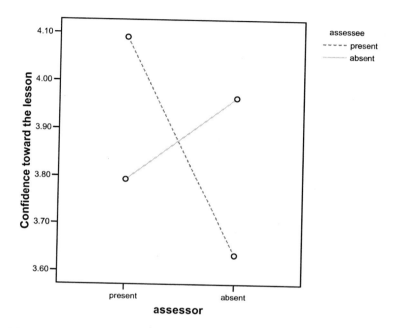

Figure 4.2 Confidence toward the lesson

To test hypothesis 2-3 (differences among conditions), another quantitative analysis (one-factor MANOVA by condition) was conducted. According to the multiple comparisons between each two conditions, there was no significant difference in confidence among conditions. However, of relevance is that the Both-roles condition showed significantly higher score than the No-role condition and the Assessor-only role condition (see Table 4.15).

Table 4.15 Group comparisons

Dependent measure	Group		Mean difference (I-J)	SD	P	95% CI	
	(I)	(J)				Lower	Upper
Relevance	Both-roles	No-role	.6029	.1920	.012	0.09989	1.1068
		Assessor-only role	.5469	.1870	.023	0.05597	1.0378

Of the 82 participants who responded to the question regarding attitude toward the Inspiration lesson, 64 provided their opinion about what they liked the most regarding the Inspiration lesson. Two raters classified their qualitative responses into five emergent categories (see Table 4.16). Cohen's Kappa of inter-rater agreement for nominal scale is .85. According to the results of qualitative analyses, many students cited that the Inspiration lesson was helpful to organize their ideas and it would be useful in their future career (e.g., "I think I can make logical lesson plans by using Inspiration") across the conditions. In addition, students also indicated a different teaching way of Inspiration lesson was good (e.g., "I like different use of program and different class activity such as peer assessment"). Although the students who were in the control condition did not implement peer assessment, they used assessment criteria to revise their own assignment. All conditions showed a similar frequency pattern for each of the coding categories. Accordingly, chi-square analyses revealed no significant differences among the frequencies represented by these categories.

Table 4.16 Percentages of categorical responses for MOST liked aspect of the Inspiration lesson

Category of response	Condition			
	No-role (n=17)	Assessor-only role (n=16)	Assessee-only role (n=16)	Both-roles (n=15)
The Inspiration lesson is easy	6%	6%	6%	14%
The Inspiration lesson is fun	24%	18%	12%	7%
The Inspiration lesson is helpful for the future	30%	42%	36%	49%
The Inspiration lesson has different program and different	36%	24%	24%	28%

teaching way				
Other	4%	8%	22%	2%

The students who responded to the previous open-ended question about the Inspiration lesson also provided their opinion about what they liked least about the Inspiration lesson. Two raters classified their responses into five emergent categories (see Table 4.17). Cohen's Kappa of inter-rater agreement for nominal scale is .82. According to the results of qualitative analyses, many students felt Inspiration lesson was somewhat difficult and tedious (e.g., "I am not good at making concept map and it is laborious and time-consuming") across the conditions. The students in the Both-roles conditions were more likely to report that peer assessment required extra efforts than the students in the other conditions. All the four conditions showed a relatively similar frequency pattern for each of the coding categories. For this reason, chi-square analyses revealed no significant differences among the frequencies represented by these categories.

Table 4.17 Percentages of categorical responses for LEAST liked aspect of the Inspiration lesson

Category of response	Condition			
	No-role (n=14)	Assessor-only role (n=14)	Assessee-only role (n=15)	Both-roles (n=15)
The Inspiration lesson is difficult	14%	21%	42%	30%
Technical problems bother me	28%	35%	6%	12%
The assignment is tedious and time-consuming	42%	21%	30%	42%
The Inspiration lesson needs extra effort for peer assessment	0%	7%	6%	12%
Other	16%	16%	16%	4%

Motivation toward the peer assessment activities. Since the control condition did not implement peer assessment activities, a one-factor MANOVA was conducted to test hypothesis

2-3 (motivation toward peer assessment), with four sub-dependent measures including attention, relevance, competence, and satisfaction. The one factor MANOVA indicated that there was an overall effect of different conditions on motivation toward the peer assessment activities, Wilks Lambda=.756, F(8,114)=2.138, p<.05, η^2 =.175. ANOVA indicated that significant differences occurred in attention, F(2,60)=3.446, p<.05, η^2 =.105, and confidence, F(2,60)=5.673, p<.05, η^2 =.161.

Post-hoc test of all pair-wise comparisons for attention and confidence were conducted through Tukey HSD procedure. Of all comparisons, Assessor's role (M=3.12, SD=.70) versus Assessee's role (M=3.65, SD=.66) had significant mean difference in the attention toward peer assessment. On the contrary, Both-roles condition (M=3.98, SD=.94) had higher mean than the Assessee-only role condition (M=3.08, SD=.98) for the confidence toward peer assessment.

Of the 63 participants in the three treatment conditions, 52 provided their opinion about what they most liked about the peer assessment activities. Two raters classified their qualitative responses into emerging five categories (see Table 4.18). Cohen's Kappa of inter-rater agreement for nominal scale is .83. According to the results of qualitative analyses, many students thought peer assessment was helpful to enhance their own learning (e.g., "it made me think about what I should do in my assignment"). They also liked seeing other's perspectives (e.g., "I like to evaluate someone else's work because I can see their ideas") whether they played the assessor's role, the assessee's role or both roles. However, students showed different attitudes toward peer feedback. Specifically, the students who played a role of assessor liked critical peer feedback or anonymous peer feedback, while the students who played a role of assessee liked positive peer feedback. Despite this interesting difference, chi-square analyses revealed no significant differences among the frequencies represented by these categories.

Table 4.18 Percentages of categorical responses for MOST liked aspect of peer assessment

Category of response	Condition		
	Assessor-only role (n=16)	Assessee-only role (n=16)	Both-roles (n=15)
Peer assessment is helpful to	40%	43%	25%

improve my assignment			
I like positive peer feedback	0%	13%	42%
I like anonymous and critical peer feedback	12%	0%	13%
I like seeing other's perspectives	35%	25%	13%
Other	16%	19%	7%

The students who responded to previous open-ended question about the peer assessment activities also provided their opinion about what they least liked about peer assessment. Two raters classified their responses into emerging five categories (see Table 4.19). Cohen's Kappa of inter-rater agreement for nominal scale is .82. According to the results of qualitative analyses, many students reported peer feedback was superficial and not in-depth enough to enhance their learning. This opinion was more common among the students who played a role of assessee that among the students who played a role of assessor. However, many students cited that giving or receiving critical feedback is difficult, whether they played an assessor' role or assessee's role. In addition, they doubted their own ability as assessors as well as their peers' ability to provide useful feedback. Since the three treatment conditions did not show notable difference in their responses, chi-square analyses revealed no significant differences among the frequencies represented by these categories.

Table 4.19 Percentages of categorical responses for LEAST like aspect of the peer assessment

	Condition		
Category of response	Assessor-only role (n=14)	Assessee-only role (n=12)	Both-roles (n=14)
Peer feedback is superficial	14%	41%	28%
Giving or receiving critical feedback is hard	14%	17%	28%
Peer assessment is time-consuming	28%	17%	7%
Peer's quality or my own quality is not enough to give useful feedback	7%	17%	21%

73

Others	37%	8%	16%

Examination of Additional Data about Hypotheses 3

This section describes the additional analyses for the relationship between the quality of peer assessment activities and the dependent variables. Specifically, the relationship between peer feedback score and back-feedback score and each dependent variable was investigated.

Peer Feedback Score

From the aspect of Assessee, the correlation between received peer feedback score and dependent variables was tested. The correlation between peer feedback score and assessee's metacognitive awareness was not significant. The correlation between peer feedback score and performance or attitude was also not significant.

Back-feedback Score

From the aspect of Assessee, the correlation between back-feedback score (score range 0-5: higher score implies more agreement to peer's feedback) and the dependent variables were tested. Only the correlation between back-feedback score and assessee's performance score was significant at the 0.01 level ($r = -.493$). This indicates that assesses who showed less agreement to peer feedback performed better in their assignment.

Summary of the Hypotheses Tests

This section clarifies the results of the tested hypotheses for each of the three research questions based on the statistical tests presented in previous sections. All of above statistical test results are summarized in Table 4.20.

Table 4.20 Summary of statistical test results

Dependent Variable	Measures	By Main Effects				By Condition			
		Assessor's role absent	present	Assessee's role absent	Present	No-role	Assessor-only role	Assessee-only role	Both-roles
Metacognitive Awareness	Change in perspective	N/A	N/A	N/A	N/A	N/A			
	Self-reported regulatory skills								
	1. planning			**Main effect** (absent < present)			Sig. (No-role < Assessee-only role) Sig. (No-role < Both-roles)		
	2. Information management								
	3. Monitoring								
	4. Debugging								
	5. Evaluation			**Main effect** (absent < present)			Sig. (No-role < Both-roles)		
Performance	Assignment score								
	1. Objective score			**Main effect** (absent < present) **Interaction effect** (Asessor only & Assessee only > Both & Control)			Sig. (No-role < Assessor-only role) Sig. (No-role < Assessee-only role)		
	2. Subjective score								
Attitude	Toward the lesson								
	1. Attention								
	2. Relevance						Sig. (No-role < Both- roles) Sig. (Assessor-only role < Both-roles)		
	3. Confidence			**Interaction effect** (Asessor only & Assessee only < Both & Control)					
	4. Satisfaction								
	Toward peer assessment								
	1. Attention	N/A	N/A	N/A	N/A	N/A	Sig. (Assessor < Assessee)		
	2. Relevance	N/A	N/A	N/A	N/A	N/A			
	3. Confidence	N/A	N/A	N/A	N/A	N/A	Sig. (Assessee < Both-roles)		
	4. Satisfaction	N/A	N/A	N/A	N/A	N/A			

Correlation study:
- Back feedback score and Assessee's performance were significantly correlated negatively.

Hypotheses 1

Hypotheses 1 addressed research question 1, "What are the comparative effects of Assessor's role and Assessee's role on metacognitive awareness, performance, and attitude?"

Hypothesis 1-1. The students who play either the Assessor's role or Assessee's role will show higher metacognitive awareness than the students who do not play either of the roles. In addition, the students who play an Assessor's role will show greater metacognitive awareness than the students who play an Assessee's role.

The results of the test. According to an analysis by main effect, the main effect of the Assessee's role was significant. In other words, the students who played a role of Assessee showed significantly higher metacognitive awareness (specifically, in planning and evaluation) than the students who did not played a role of Assessee. However, the main effect of the Assessor's role was not significant.

According to an additional analysis by condition, there was no significant difference between the students who played an Assessor-only role and the students who played an Assessee-only role in metacognitive awareness. Therefore, the hypothesis 1-1 was partially supported.

Hypothesis 1-2. The students who play either the Assessor's role or the Assessee's role will show higher performance than the students who do not play either of the roles. However, there will be no difference between the students who play the Assessor's role and the students who play the Assessee's role in performance for the technology-related design task.

The results of the test. The main effect of the Assessee's role was significant. In other words, the students who played an Assessee role showed significantly higher performance (specifically, in objective score) than the students who did not play an Assessee role. On the contrary, the main effect of the Assessor's role was not significant. However, the interaction effect of the Assessor's role and the Assessee's role was significant. Specifically, the students who were in only one role conditions (Assessor's role only & Assessee's role only) showed significantly higher performance than the students in Both-roles condition or No-role condition.

76

According to an additional analysis by condition, the Assessor's role condition and the Assessee's role condition did not show significant difference in performance. Therefore, the hypothesis 1-2 was also supported partially.

Hypothesis 1-3. The students who play either an Assessor's role or an Assessee's role will show more positive attitude toward the lesson than the students who will not play either of the roles. The students who play an Assessor's role will show more positive attitude toward peer assessment than the students who play an Assessee's role.

The results of the test. There was no main effect of the two roles in student's attitude toward the lesson. Moreover, according to an additional analysis by condition, the student in Assessee's role condition showed significantly better attitude toward the peer assessment (especially, in attention) than the students in Assessor's role condition. Thus, hypothesis 1-3 was not supported by the test results.

Hypotheses 2

Hypotheses 2 addressed the research question 2, "Does the combination of playing both the assessor's role and assessee's role improve learner's metacognitive awareness, performance, and attitude than either of the role alone or neither role?"

Hypothesis 2-1. The students taking both roles (playing both the Assessor's role and Assessee' role) will show greater metacognitive awareness than the students who take either of the roles alone or the students who are in the control group.

The results of the test. There was no interaction effect of the two roles. In addition, there is no significant difference between the Both-roles condition and only one-role conditions. However, the Both-roles condition showed significantly higher score than no role (control) condition in self-reported regulatory skills (specifically, in planning and evaluation). Accordingly, hypothesis 2-1 was supported partially.

Hypothesis 2-2. The students playing both roles (assessor's role + assessee's role) will show greater performance than the students who take either of the roles alone or the students who are in the control group.

The results of the tests. According to the interaction effect of the Assessor's role and the Assessee's role on performance (specifically, in object aspect score), the students who played only one role performed significantly better than the students in Both-roles condition or control condition (No-role). Therefore, the hypothesis 2-2 was not supported.

Hypothesis 2-3. The students playing both roles (assessor's role + assessee's role) will indicate a more positive attitude toward the lesson and the peer assessment activities than students who play either role alone or no role (control group).

The results of the tests. In testing attitude toward the lesson, the interaction effect of the Assessor's role and the Assessee's role was significant for confidence. Specifically, the Both-roles condition and the control condition showed higher confidence to the lesson than the students who played only one role. However, there was no significant difference between Both-roles condition and control condition. Both-roles condition showed significant higher score than Assessor-only role condition and control condition with respect to relevance.

In testing attitude toward the peer assessment, the Both-roles condition showed significant higher score than Assessee's role condition in competence. Accordingly, hypothesis 2-3 was partially supported.

Hypotheses 3

Hypotheses 3 addressed research question 3, "Are there any relationships between the quality of peer feedback or back-feedback and Assessees' performance, attitude, and metacognitive awareness?

Hypothesis 3-1. Assessees who receive high quality peer feedback will show better metacognitive awareness, performance, and positive attitude than Assessees who receive low quality peer feedback.

78

The results of the test. Correlation analyses did not show any significant correlation between the quality of peer feedback and three dependent variables of Assessees. Accordingly, the hypothesis 3-1 was not supported.

Hypothesis 3-2. Assessees who compose positive back-feedback (high back-feedback score) will show better metacognitive awareness, performance, and attitude than Assessees who compose negative back-feedback (low back-feedback score).

The results of the test. Correlation analyses showed that back-feedback score and Assessee's performance was significantly associated, but negatively. This result was on the opposite side of the hypothesis 3-2. Therefore, the hypothesis was not supported.

CHAPTER V

DISCUSSION

This chapter provides a summary of the results of the study and a discussion to interpret the meaning of these results. Next, the implications and limitations of the study are discussed. Finally, suggestions for future research and a brief conclusion are presented.

Summary of Results & Its Interpretation

This study examined the effects of two types of student's role (Assessor's role or Assessee's role) in peer assessment on metacognitive awareness, performance, and attitude. In the following sub-sections, results and their interpretation are presented. Specifically, interpretations about the results of the testing of hypotheses 1 (the comparative effects of the Assessor's role and the Assessee's role), hypotheses 2 (the effects of the Assessor's role + Assessee's role), and hypotheses 3 (the relationship of peer feedback quality/back-feedback quality and dependent variables) are presented.

The Comparative Effects of the Assessor's role and the Assessee's role

The interpretations about the comparative effects of the Assessor's role and Assessee's role are presented in the following sections.

Metacognitive awareness. The effects on metacognitive awareness were measured by two aspects: (1) change perspective of the value of peer assessment and (2) self-reported regulatory skills. There was no significant difference in change perspective of the value of peer assessment. Although the descriptive data showed a little higher score in Assessor-only role condition than in Assessee-only role condition, the difference was not statistically significant. One possible reason may be found in students' open-ended answers. According to the students' answers to the open-ended question asking the reason for their response, many students reported that peer assessment experience during the lesson was very superficial. Since there was a the lack of the amount of time allowed for the peer assessment activities, students seemed to not be involved enough in peer assessment to understand the meaning of peer assessment as a learning method.

In self-reported regulatory skills, the main effect of the Assessor's role was not significant. This result is inconsistent with current studies reporting the effectiveness of Assessor's role on self-reflection (Blom & Poole, 2004; Topping et al., 2000). One of the possible reasons may be the same reason as mentioned above, the lack of in-depth experience.

On the contrary, the main effect of the Assessee's role was significant. In other words, the students who played a role of Assessee showed significantly higher self-reported regulatory skills (specifically, in planning and evaluation) than the students who did not played a role of Assessee. As there is no study reporting empirical evidence of the effects of Assessee's role on metacognitive awareness, interpreting the unique results is difficult. However, this finding may be explained by the back-feedback activity for Assessee. In this study, the students who played a role of Assessee had an opportunity to review peer's feedback by filling out back-feedback form, while most of the current peer assessment studies simply consider Assessee's role as only receiving peer feedback. Through the activity of filling out back-feedback form, the Assessees might have an in-depth chance to review their own learning process. As a result, the Assessee paid more attention to planning for the revising Inspiration assignment and to evaluating their revised assignment. This result is meaningful because there was little empirical evidence to support that peer assessment offers students the opportunity to reflect upon the learning process, as well as the assessment process, especially from an Assessee's perspective.

Performance. The effects on performance were measured by two aspects: (1) objective score and (2) subjective score. In the objective score, the main effect of the Assessor's role was not significant. It means that assessing peer's assignment was not quite helpful for the students who played a role of Assessor to improve their own learning. This result is contradictory to other research reporting the effectiveness of the Assessor's role on performance (Kim, 2003; Topping et al., 2000; Tsai et al., 2002). One of the possible reasons for the result can be found in current studies about peer assessment criteria (Miller, 2003; Orsmond et al., 1996; Rust et al., 2003). According to these studies, one factor decreasing the effectiveness of peer assessment is students' lack of understanding of assessment criteria. From the same context, the result of this study may be explained. Although the students assessed peer's assignment with subjective criteria, the experience did not help much the students' own learning because they did not thoroughly understand the assessment criteria. For this reason, the experience of assessing did not seem to be helpful for the students to revise their own assignment. Another reason may be found in the study and class circumstance. Since the experiment was very tightly scheduled, the students might have no chance to reflect thoroughly upon the assessment criteria.

On the contrary, the main effect of the Assessee's role was significant. In other words, the students who played a role of Assessee showed significantly higher performance (specifically, in objective score) than the students who did not play a role of Assessee. This finding may be explained also by the back-feedback activity for Assessees. Although the Assessees used the same amount of time to review peer's feedback and to fill out the back-feedback form as the Assessors spent to assess peer's assignment, the Assessees might understand more clearly the assessment criteria by comparing the received peer feedback with back-feedback criteria. This also could be attributed to the fact that the Assessees simply received more feedback to use to improve their assignment

However, in the subjective score, there were no significant results. This result may be related to the characteristics of assessment criteria. Specifically, in the objective assessment criteria, the students might easily detect which aspect of their assignment should be improved because the criteria were about objective aspects, such as required number of nodes, image, and web link (whether the students were Assessors or Assessees). In contrast, the subjective criteria might be difficult to understand the meaning of criteria. For example, "The concept map has a good coherent and logical structure." For this reason, Assessors could not give sufficient feedback to their peer, and Assessees did not receive clear feedback about their assignment in subjective assessment part. This reasoning is based on the open-ended answers of a couple of students who played Assessor's role. They said, "The subjective criteria were not clear to me," and "I was confused in choosing the best description that matches my peer's assignment quality, because the subject criteria was vague." Accordingly, when they used subjective assessment criteria, the Assessors and the Assessees did not obtain any kind of benefits of experiencing peer assessment.

Attitude. The effects on attitude were measured by two aspects: (1) motivation toward the lesson and (2) motivation toward the peer assessment. There were no significant differences between playing the Assessor's role and Assessee's role upon students' motivation toward the Inspiration lesson.

On the contrary, regarding motivation (specifically, in attention) toward peer assessment, the students in Assessee-only role condition reported significantly higher motivation (attention) than the students in Assessor-only role condition. This result is in direct contradiction to what was predicted in Hypothesis1-3: that the students who play an Assessor's role will show more positive attitude toward peer assessment than the students who play an Assessee's role. The hypothesis was based on some studies that reported Assessees' skeptical attitude toward peer feedback (McDowell, 1995; Orsmond et al., 1996).

However, if we carefully observe the result of this study, we can realize it is not quite the opposite result of the hypothesis. In this study, the Assessees showed significantly higher score in attention toward peer assessment than the Assessors. The reason may be found in Assessees' open-ended opinions. According to the students' opinions about peer assessment, which were the answers to the open-ended questions asking good aspects and bad aspects of peer assessment, Assessees showed their concerns about peer's critical feedback and peer's ability to assess their assignment. This kind of concern may be enough to attract Assessee's attention. Therefore, although the apparent result is different, the core meaning coincides with the hypothesis. The primary difference is that current studies focused on a general attitude toward peer assessment, while this study focused on a specific attitude in terms of four areas of motivation.

But also this result can be explained by a totally different perspective. According to Garcia & Pintrich (1991), levels of motivation are associated with the level of cognitive

83

engagement and performance. From this perspective of the relationship between motivation and performance, assesses probably reported more motivation (attention) because they actually performed better.

The Effects of the Combination Role (Assessor' role + Assessee's role)

The results about the effects of the combination role (playing both roles: assessor's role + assessee's role) are discussed in the following sections.

Metacognitive awareness. There was no significant difference in change perspective of the value of peer assessment. Although it was not statistically significant, the Both-roles condition showed a lower score than other conditions (Assessor-only role condition and Assessee-only role condition) in descriptive data of change of perspective of the value of peer assessment.

In self-reported regulatory skills (specifically, in planning and evaluation), the Both-roles condition showed a higher score than other three conditions. However, it showed statistically significance only between the Both-roles condition and No-role (control) condition. It means playing the assessor's role and assessee's role at the same time was more helpful for students to plan and evaluate their own learning than not playing any roles.

However, playing the two roles was not significantly beneficial to students than playing only one role. This result was on the same line with students' opinion about the reason why they did not change their perspective of the value of peer assessment. Many students said that peer assessment was helpful to enhance understanding of their own learning process, but that it was superficial. To be exact, the students in Both-roles condition agreed with this opinion more than the students in other conditions. The result may be explained by the lack of sufficient time for the two roles. Although the students in Both-roles condition participated in the two types of activities ((1) assessing and giving feedback, and (2) receiving peer feedback and giving back-feedback), the amount of time allotted for the two activities was not twice as long as the other conditions' time. This was to control a time effect among conditions. Therefore, without sufficient internalizing process, simply playing both roles may not guarantee better reflection on the meaning of peer assessment and their own learning process than playing only one role.

Performance. In objective score, the findings showed opposite results of hypothesis 2-2. Hypothesis 2-2 was established based on the synergy effect of two groups of current studies: one group of studies is about the beneficial effects of assessing activity on performance (O'Donnell et al., 1986; Topping et al., 2000; Tsai et al., 2002) and the other group of studies is about the effects of receiving feedback on performance (Bangert-Drowns et al., 1991; Keig, 2000). However, the data of this study showed playing either of the roles alone promoted better performance than playing both roles.

The same reason mentioned in the previous section may also explain this result: students reported that although they recognized peer assessment was useful to understand peer's perspectives and to reflect upon their own learning, they perceived that peer assessment was superficial. There are a couple of possible reasons for this finding. The first possible reason is due to a lack of in-depth peer feedback or a lack of peer interaction. Through the investigation of the peer feedback, the researcher found that most peer assessors' feedback only indicated what was wrong, without providing suggestions for the improvement of the assessees' work. In addition, even if the assessor and assessee had different ideas about the assessee's work or assessor's feedback, they had no chance to discuss the different ideas. For these reasons, the students might perceive that the peer assessment was superficial.

The amount of time allowed for Both-role conditions may be also another possible reason for the test results. In this study, the time for peer assessment activities was limited by a tight class schedule. As the students might not have sufficient time for the peer assessment activities, they were not likely to internalize the peer assessment activities for their learning. This is particularly true for the students in Both-roles condition, because they had more activities (assessing peer's work, receiving peer feedback, and filling out back-feedback form) to complete during the allotted time than the students in other conditions.

Attitude. With respect to motivation toward the Inspiration lesson, the students who played both roles showed a more confident attitude toward the lesson than the students who played only one role. In addition, the students in Both-roles condition perceived the Inspiration lesson to be more relevant to their learning goal or future purpose than the students in No-role condition and Assessor-only role condition. These results imply that as the students experienced more peer assessment activities, they came to know better how these peer assessment activities were related to their learning goals or study purposes, and finally, they became more confident.

A similar result was found with respect to student motivation toward peer assessment. In confidence toward peer assessment, the students who played both roles showed significantly more confidence than the students who played the assessee's role alone. While the students who gave and received peer feedback in the Both-roles condition came to feel more confident, the students who only received peer feedback in Assessee-only role condition reported much lower confidence. The results may be explained by the characteristics of two activities. Receiving peer feedback sometimes encourages Assessees when providing positive feedback, but it sometimes discourages Assessees when providing negative feedback. In contrast, many studies reported that giving peer feedback often helps students' motivation due to the ownership of assessment in many cases (Ballantyne et al., 2002; Blom & Poole, 2004; Falchikov, 1995). Although some students in Both-roles condition might also receive negative peer feedback, this type of negative attitude was likely to be reduced by playing both roles simultaneously because playing both roles at a time is beneficial to understand another's perspective.

The Relationship between Peer Feedback Quality/Back-Feedback Quality and Dependent Variables

Hypothesis 3-1, Assessees who receive high quality peer feedback will show better metacognitive awareness, performance, and a more positive attitude than Assessees who receive low quality peer feedback, was not supported by the data. This result may be explained by two aspects. One possible reason is students' skeptical attitude toward their peer's ability, which is indicated by many other studies (McDowell, 1995; Orsmond et al., 1996). For this reason, the Assesses might not internalize peer feedback. Although the Assessees performed better than the Assessors in this study, it may not be the effects of peer feedback. Another possible reason is that the difference of the quality of peer feedback across students was very trivial (M=5.9, SD=.53). Accordingly, the correlation study might not show meaningful results.

On the contrary, correlation analysis showed that back-feedback score and Assessee's performance was significantly associated, but negatively. In other words, the Assessees who composed more negative back-feedback (low back-feedback score) showed better performance than the Assessees who composed more positive back-feedback. Interesting things were found through in-depth investigation of back-feedback. According to the investigation, most Assessees who composed more negative back-feedback tended to provide more specific and logical reasons for their marks than the other Assessees. From this context, it can be inferred that the students who provided good rationale seem to better understand the assessment criteria or the requirement of the assignment than the students who provided insufficient rationales. Thorough understanding of the requirement of the assignment might help the students not only better perform their assignment, but also express their opinion in a clear and critical manner.

Summary of Interpretation

In comparative effects of the two roles, the data presented suggested that the Assessee's role was helpful for students to enhance metacognitive awareness on their own learning and to promote their performance, while the assessor's role did not show significant effectiveness. It may be explained by the back-feedback activity for Assessees, which seems to help Assessees internalize peer feedback.

In the effects of combination role (playing both roles: assessor's role + assessee's role), the Both-roles condition did not always outperform the Assessor-only role condition or Assessee-only role condition. Contrary to what had been hypothesized, the one role only conditions sometimes outperformed the Both-roles condition. The results of this study illustrated that simply playing two different roles at a time does not always guarantee better effects of peer assessment than playing only one role. Even when students play only one role during peer assessment, they can have benefits of peer assessment for their learning.

The relationship between back-feedback score and Assessee's performance was significantly associated, but negatively. It may be explained by the degree of students' understanding of the assessment criteria and the requirements of the assignment. By the assesses critiquing their peer's feedback, it seems to have empowered them to have better understand the criteria and prove their own performance.

Limitation of the Study

Several limitations of this study must be considered. First, this study did not fulfill the conditions of the random selection of the sample from the population (preservice teachers). Since the participants were not randomly selected from a specific population, the population group to which the research finding should be generalized is more limited. This limitation caused a problem in determining the external validity of the current study.

Second, an internal validity issue might be raised by unexpected technical problems. Due to technical problems during peer assessment activities, such as failing to upload or download assignment files, students might report more negative attitudes toward peer assessment or the lesson. This contamination was realized by students' open-ended answers in the attitude survey. According to some students' opinions, they disliked peer assessment due to tedious technical problems.

Third, the results of this study were reported based on the findings of only one-time experiment. For this reason, it is not easy to say that the results of this study are reliable. In addition, as there was no similar study to this study dealing with role effect in peer assessment, these findings should be interpreted cautiously.

Fourth, there were a lot of time constraints during the experiment, because it was conducted in a regular class session of one and half hours. Only twenty minutes were allowed for peer assessment activity (giving or receiving feedback). This is likely to have limited learning among the students experiencing a new learning method. In addition, students might not have had enough time for training for peer assessment activities and pre/post intervention surveys.

Fifth, although this study specified the effects of peer assessment on metacognitive awareness and motivation by presenting every individual effect on each sub-construct, this study did not provide in-depth investigation on the individual effects. For example, the results of this study reported Assessee's role's main effect in two sub-areas of metacognitive awareness (planning and evaluation). However, it tried to explain the results only from a large boundary of metacognitive awareness rather than from the sub-areas.

Finally, the results of this study were mainly based on quantitative data. Although several open-ended answers were collected by surveys, those answers were not enough to obtain students' actual and in-depth perception. Moreover, since the open-ended questions were too broad (e.g., what did you like Most/Least about peer assessment?), students' answers to the questions were very general and did not show any kind of significant difference between conditions.

Implications

The findings of this study may suggest instructional implications for those who want to apply the idea of learning by assessing or learning by receiving feedback in a several ways.

First, since this study presented specific effects of peer assessment from the Assessee's aspect as well as Assessor's aspect, it may enable researchers and/or practitioners to review the comparative effects of the two roles on the particular dependent variables. By comparing the concrete effects of the two roles on metacognitive awareness, performance, and attitude, these reviews will be helpful for them to design proper practice of peer assessment.

Second, this study tried to measure the effects of Assessor's role and Assessee's role on various dependent measures. As this study specified the sub-areas of each dependent variable, such as the five sub-constructs of metacognitive awareness and the four sub-constructs for motivation, the findings may provide more specific and tangible instructional implications for future researchers or practitioners to apply the findings to their particular interested area. For example, if a teacher wants to increase students' metacognitive awareness, he can assign a more effective role to his students based on interest areas. Specifically, if the teacher wants to increase students' planning skill through peer assessment, he can assign assessee's role to his students, and if he wants to increase evaluation skill, playing both roles can be recommended based on the results of this study. Especially, since empirical study about metacognitive awareness is very rare, the results of this study will be helpful to give a rough understanding of the effects of the two roles on metacognitive awareness.

Third, this study may provide ideas concerning well-developed criteria. In performance, it was found that subjective assessment criteria were not as useful because of students' lack of understanding of the meaning of assessment criteria even after training. In contrast, students easily understood objective assessment criteria and they improved their assignment based on the objective criteria. Therefore, the finding implies developing clear and specific assessment is important. It confirms the results of current studies stating the effectiveness of well-developed assessment criteria (Bloxham & West, 2004; Kim, 2003; Miller, 2003; Orsmond et al., 1996; Orsmond et al., 2000; Rust et al., 2003; Sluijsmans et al., 2002; Woolf, 2004).

Fourth, this study may give ideas about well-designed role activity in peer assessment. According to the overall results of this study, the Assessee's role was more effective in various dependent measures than Assessor's role. This result was unexpected because many current studies have reported the effects of Assessor's role in peer assessment. One of the possible explanations of the result may be found in back-feedback activity. While most current practices and research considered Assessee's role as only receiving peer feedback, this study considered it as reflecting their learning through back-feedback activity as well as receiving peer feedback by providing the back-feedback activity, which helped Assessee reflect their own learning. In this study, back-feedback activity seemed to endow the Assessees with the assessor's role. And they were even more motivated to be Assessors because they were assessing those that assessed them. It implies that the effects of well-designed role activity may exceed typical benefits from the role.

Further Research

The results of this study suggest several directions for future research. First, a true experimental design is desired for more generalizable research finding. Although conducting a true experiment study is not easy, the results will be more powerful.

Second, the same study through automated peer assessment supporting system is recommended for desirable future research. Due to technical problems during peer assessment, such as failing to upload or download assignment files, students might report a more negative attitude toward peer assessment or the lesson. In addition, many students said one of challenges of practicing peer assessment in the classroom is the extra amount of time required. Using automated supporting systems for peer assessment might solve this issue, because automated systems may help students and instructors reduce their time for peer assessment practice.

Third, in-depth investigation on the effects of two types of roles in peer assessment on each sub-construct of metacognitive awareness and motivation is recommended. Although this study presented the effects of peer assessment on specific areas of metacognitive awareness and motivation by showing the effects on each sub-construct, it did not provide in-depth investigation on the individual effects.

Fourth, similar studies should be conducted to verify the findings of this study. Since this study was unique in two aspects: (1) it investigated the effects of two different roles in peer assessment and (2) it was an empirical study dealing with metacognition issues in peer assessment, it is difficult to compare the results of this study with those of other studies. Thus, much more similar studies should be conducted to verify the results of this study.

Fifth, a duplicated study is recommended to be conducted by different data collecting methods. In this study, the researcher used mainly quantitative data collection method for each dependent variable. Although several open-ended answers were collected by survey, those answers were not enough to obtain students' real perception. Therefore, to collect greater depth data, a qualitative approach is recommended.

Finally, more interactive peer assessment study among students is recommended. In this study, the back-feedback assessed by Assessees was not delivered Assessors. However, if the researcher gave the back-feedback to Assessors or provided a discussion opportunity between Assessors and Assessees, the results might be different from current findings. As interaction is one of important factors stimulating students' learning, peer interaction is necessary to maximize the effectiveness of peer assessment as a learning method.

Conclusion

This study investigated the effects of Assessor's role and Assessee's role on metacognitive awareness, performance, and attitude. Based on the present findings, the researcher can conclude the following.

In comparative effects of the two roles, the data presented suggested that the Assessee's role was helpful for students to enhance metacognitive awareness on their own learning and to promote their performance, while the Assessor's role did not show significant effectiveness. In the effects of combination role (Assessor's role + Assessee's role), the Both-roles condition did not always outperform the Assessor's only role condition or Assessee's only role condition. Contrary to what had been hypothesized, the only one role conditions sometimes outperformed the Both-roles condition. The results of this study illustrated that simply playing two different roles at a time does not always guarantee the effects of peer assessment. In other words, although students play only one role during peer assessment, they can have a lot of benefits for their learning from the only one role.

The results of this study does not seem to support major current studies of peer assessment that have mainly reported the beneficial effects of Assessor's role (Blom & Pool, 2004; Kim, 2004; Tsai, et al., 2002). However, this study does not indicate that the Assessor's role was not effective, but indicates that the Assessee's role may also have a lot of beneficial effects on students' learning, particularly when they are given opportunity to provide back-feedback. Due to a lack of understanding about the effects of Assessee's role, we can not explain the overall effects of peer assessment on students learning. In addition, we realized that simply adding the two different roles does not always guarantee the effectiveness of peer assessment. On the contrary, we may infer an important instructional implication through the effectiveness of objective assessment criteria and back-feedback activity: well-developed assessment criteria and well-designed role activity may contribute to the effectiveness of a certain role in peer assessment.

Due to the lack of fully randomized design and the short treatment time, the results and interpretation might be exploratory and tentative. Therefore, some further studies that can verify the results are recommended.

APPENDIX A

SAMPLE STUDENT CONCEPT MAP

SAMPLE STUDENT CONCEPT MAP

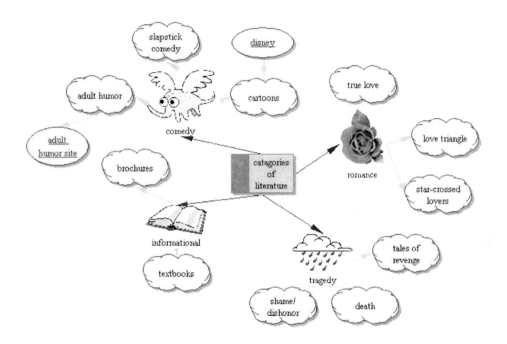

APPENDIX B

PEER ASSESSMENT FORM

PEER ASSESSMENT FORM

(Use this form when you assess peer's draft)

Last 4 digit of SSN:

1. Objective part

- For each criterion, mark yes or no.
- After marking, write comments or notes.

Features	Yes	No	Comments/Notes
Minimum 12 nodes			
Lines, arrows, text in lines			
Different shapes and images			
At least one external image via the Symbol Palette			
At least one web link			

2. Subjective part

- For each of four criteria, choose the description that best matches the student work.
- After choosing one description, write the reason why you chose the description.

2-1. Clarity of Structure

Check One	☐ The concept map has a good coherent and logical structure ☐ Some parts are not coherent or logical, but overall the structure are understandable ☐ Most parts are not logical or coherent.

- Why do you think so?

2-2. Completeness

Check One	☐ The concept map covers all of the relevant topics and issues ☐ Although a couple of topics and issues are missing, the concept map covers overall topic and issue ☐ The concept map does not cover most key topics and issues

- Why do you think so?

2-3. Support	
Check One	☐ The concept map includes an appropriate amount of supporting materials such as graphics and notes ☐ Although the concept map does not provide enough supportive materials, the author's ideas are well supported ☐ The concept map provides too much or too little support materials
▪ Why do you think so?	

2-4. Creativity	
Check One	☐ The concept map has a lot of unique aspects expressing the author's creative ideas ☐ The concept map expresses the author's ideas with just a few creative aspects. ☐ The concept map expresses the author's ideas in a very ordinary way
▪ Why do you think so?	

APPENDIX B-1

SAMPLE STUDENT PEER ASSESSMENT FORM

PEER ASSESSMENT FORM *(SAMPLE)*

(Use this form when you assess peer's draft)

Last 4 digit of SSN: __0734__

1. Objective part

- For each criterion, mark yes or no.
- After marking, write comments or notes.

Features	Yes	No	Comments/Notes
Minimum 12 nodes	v		
Lines, arrows, text in lines	v		
Different shapes and images	v		Great use of images
At least one external image via the Symbol Palette	v		
At least one web link		V	

2. Subjective part

- For each of four criteria, choose the description that best matches the student work.
- After choosing one description, write the reason why you chose the description.

2-1. Clarity of Structure

Check One	■ The concept map has a good coherent and logical structure ☐ Some parts are not coherent or logical, but overall the structure are understandable ☐ Most parts are not logical or coherent.

- Why do you think so?

There is a main point in the middle and different ideas branching off.
Easy to follow

2-2. Completeness

Check One	☐ The concept map covers all of the relevant topics and issues ■ Although a couple of topics and issues are missing, the concept map covers overall topic and issue ☐ The concept map does not cover most key topics and issues

- Why do you think so?

Looks like every issue is covered, although not in detail

99

2-3. Support	
Check One	☐ The concept map includes an appropriate amount of supporting materials such as graphics and notes ■ Although the concept map does not provide enough supportive materials, the author's ideas are well supported ☐ The concept map provides too much or too little support materials

- Why do you think so?

Has supporting graphics, but not details

2-4. Creativity	
Check One	■ The concept map has a lot of unique aspects expressing the author's creative ideas ☐ The concept map expresses the author's ideas with just a few creative aspects. ☐ The concept map expresses the author's ideas in a very ordinary way

- Why do you think so?

I think the idea is good

APPENDIX B-2

EVALUATION FORM FOR PEER ASSESSMENT FORM

EVALUATION FORM FOR PEER ASSESSMENT FORM
(For Raters)

Last four digit numbers of Student:		
Rater:		

1. Objective Criteria		
	Yes (1)	**No (0)**
• Mark all criteria		
• Provide at least one comment		
Total score for objective criteria	/2	

2. Subjective Criteria	
2-1. Clarity of Structure	**score**
▪ **2 point**: Providing mark and feedback with rationale or specific suggestion for revision ▪ **1 point:** Providing mark and written feedback, but not clear or superficial ▪ **0 point:** Missed mark or written feedback	
2-2. Completeness	**score**
▪ **2 point**: Providing mark and feedback with rationale or specific suggestion for revision ▪ **1 point:** Providing mark and written feedback, but not clear or superficial ▪ **0 point:** Missed mark or written feedback	
2-3. Support	**score**
▪ **2 point**: Providing mark and feedback with rationale or specific suggestion for revision ▪ **1 point:** Providing mark and written feedback, but not clear or superficial ▪ **0 point:** Missed mark or written feedback	
2-4. Creativity	**score**
▪ **2 point**: Providing mark and feedback with rationale or specific suggestion for revision ▪ **1 point:** Providing mark and written feedback, but not clear or superficial ▪ **0 point:** Missed mark or written feedback	
Total score for subjective criteria	/8
Total	/10

APPENDIX B-3

TRAINING MATERIAL FOR PEER ASSESSMENT

TRAINING MATERIAL FOR PEER ASSESSMENT

The example concept map below is developed by a student. Review the concept map with given criteria in Peer Assessment Form. *(Make sure that students are given Peer Assessment Form)*

<Example concept map>

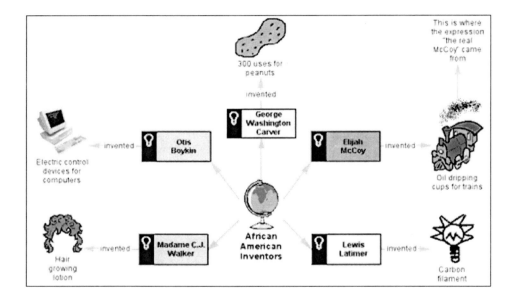

Now, I'll briefly explain the Peer Assessment Form you have. The Peer Assessment Form has five objective criteria and four subjective criteria.

The five objective criteria are (1) minimum 12 nodes, (2) line, arrows, text in lines, (3) different shapes and images, (4) at least one external image, and (5) at least one web link via four criteria.

If your peer's work has the specific feature, **(1) mark** under "Yes." If not, mark under "No." After marking, **(2) leave your short comments** in "Comments/Note" box. For example, if your peer's concept map has only 10 nodes, check under "No," then, give the reason, such as "you have only ten nodes."

The four subjective criteria are (1) clarity of structure, (2) completeness, (3) support, and (4) creativity.

- o   'Clarity of structure' requires students to construct a concept map with a good coherent and logical structure;
- o   'Completeness' requires students to create a concept map with all of the relevant topics and issues;
- o   'Support' requires students to map their ideas with appropriate amount of supportive materials;
- o   'Creativity' requires students to generate a concept map with unique aspects.

For each criterion, **(1) select one** that reflects the quality of the assignment among the three given choices (see Peer Assessment Form). Then, **(2) provide your explanation for the decision** in the open-ended question that asks the reason why they choose the description

It is time to practice. If you have any questions during the practice, let me know it.

APPENDIX C

BACK-FEEDBACK FORM

BACK-FEEDBACK FORM (FOR ASSESSEES)

Last four digit member of SSN:	Class:

1. First, carefully review your peer's feedback on your draft assignment in the peer assessment.
2. Then, for the each peer feedback, leave your opinion.

1. Objective part

- Do you agree with your peer's opinion on your draft assignment in terms of the criteria of "Objective part"?

☐ Yes, I agree   ☐ No, I disagree

- Why or why not?

2. Subjective part

2-1. Clarity of Structure

- Do you agree with your peer's opinion on your draft assignment in terms of the criteria of "Clarity of Structure"?

☐ Yes, I agree   ☐ No, I disagree

- Why or why not?

2-2. Completeness

- Do you agree with your peer's opinion on your draft assignment in terms of the criteria of "Completeness"?

☐ Yes, I agree   ☐ No, I disagree

- Why or why not?

2-3. Support

- Do you agree with your peer's opinion on your draft assignment in terms of the criteria of "Support"?

        ☐ Yes, I agree   ☐ No, I disagree

- Why or why not?

2-4. Creativity

- Do you agree with your peer's opinion on your draft assignment in terms of the criteria of "Creativity"?

        ☐ Yes, I agree   ☐ No, I disagree

- Why or why not?

APPENDIX C-1

SAMPLE STUDENT BACK-FEEDBACK FORM

BACK-FEEDBACK FORM *(SAMPLE)*

Last Four digit number of SSN : __1522__	Class:

2. First, carefully review your peer's feedback on your draft assignment in the peer assessment.
2. Then, for the each peer feedback, leave your opinion.

1. Objective part

- Do you agree with your peer's opinion on your draft assignment in terms of the criteria of "Objective part"?

    ■ Yes, I agree   ☐ No, I disagree

- Why or why not?

Yes, I did all required things except for the hyperlink.

2. Subjective part

2-1. Clarity of Structure

- Do you agree with your peer's opinion on your draft assignment in terms of the criteria of "Clarity of Structure"?

    ☐ Yes, I agree   ■ No, I disagree

- Why or why not?

I thought it was in pretty good order and understandable.

2-2. Completeness

- Do you agree with your peer's opinion on your draft assignment in terms of the criteria of "Completeness"?

    ■ Yes, I agree   ☐ No, I disagree

- Why or why not?

I covered everything. I think my structure is good

2-3. Support

- Do you agree with your peer's opinion on your draft assignment in terms of the criteria of "Support"?

☐ Yes, I agree   ▣ No, I disagree

- Why or why not?

because we need only 12 nodes. We don't need to go into much detail.

2-4. Creativity

- Do you agree with your peer's opinion on your draft assignment in terms of the criteria of "Creativity"?

▣ Yes, I agree   ☐ No, I disagree

- Why or why not?

I think adding beach whether is creative, but I've added more new.

APPENDIX C-2

EVALUATION FORM FOR BACK-FEEDBACK FORM

Evaluation Form for Back-Feedback Form

(for Raters)

Last four digit number of SSN:			
Rater:			
	Agree (1) Positive response	**Disagree (0)** Negative response	
1. Objective part			
2. Subjective part			
2-1. Clarity of structure			
2-1. Completeness			
2-3. Support			
2-4. Creativity			
		Agree/Disagree total Score	/5

Open-ended questions			
	2 point: Providing reasonable rationale for his/her opinion	**1 point:** Providing rationale for his/her opinion but not clear	**0 point:** Missed written feedback
1.Objective part			
2. Subjective part			
2-1. Clarity of Structure			
2-2. Completeness			
2-3. Support			
2-4. Creativity			
		Open-ended question quality total Score:	/10

113

APPENDIX D

METACOGNITIVE AWARENESS QUESTIONNAIRE

METACOGNITIVE AWARENESS QUESTIONNAIRE

Name:	Class:

Please answer all questions on this questionnaire.

Please answer the question with respect to the experience of assessing your peer's Inspiration assignment.

▪ The activity of assessing my peer's work changed my perspective of the value of peer assessment.	Strongly disagree	Disagree	Neutral	Agree	Strongly agree

      o Why or Why not?

Please answer all questions with respect to the experience of revising your Inspiration assignment. (Please circle one answer for each statement)

1. I thought about what I really needed to learn before I revised my Inspiration assignment.	Strongly disagree	Disagree	Neutral	Agree	Strongly agree
2. I created my own examples to make information more meaningful when I revised my Inspiration assignment.	Strongly disagree	Disagree	Neutral	Agree	Strongly agree
3. I asked myself periodically if I was meeting my goals while I revised my Inspiration assignment.	Strongly disagree	Disagree	Neutral	Agree	Strongly agree
4. I asked others for help when I don't understand something about the revision of Inspiration assignment.	Strongly disagree	Disagree	Neutral	Agree	Strongly agree
5. I summarized what I'd learned after I finished revising my Inspiration assignment.	Strongly disagree	Disagree	Neutral	Agree	Strongly agree
6. I set specific goals before I began revising my Inspiration assignment.	Strongly disagree	Disagree	Neutral	Agree	Strongly agree
7. I drew pictures or diagrams to help me understand while I revised my Inspiration assignment.	Strongly disagree	Disagree	Neutral	Agree	Strongly agree
8. I asked myself if I had considered all options when revising my Inspiration assignment.	Strongly disagree	Disagree	Neutral	Agree	Strongly agree
9. I stopped and went back over new information that was not clear during the revision of my Inspiration assignment.	Strongly disagree	Disagree	Neutral	Agree	Strongly agree

Thank you!

10. I asked myself how well I'd accomplished my goals once I finished revising my Inspiration assignment.	Strongly disagree	Disagree	Neutral	Agree	Strongly agree
11. I asked myself about the Inspiration assignment before I began revising.	Strongly disagree	Disagree	Neutral	Agree	Strongly agree
12. I focused on overall meaning rather than specifics when I revised my Inspiration assignment.	Strongly disagree	Disagree	Neutral	Agree	Strongly agree
13. I asked myself questions about how well I was doing while I was revising my Inspiration assignment.	Strongly disagree	Disagree	Neutral	Agree	Strongly agree
14. I stopped and reread when I got confused in Inspiration assignment revision.	Strongly disagree	Disagree	Neutral	Agree	Strongly agree
15. I asked myself if I had learned as much as I could have once I finished revising my Inspiration assignment.	Strongly disagree	Disagree	Neutral	Agree	Strongly agree

Thank you!

For Assessee's role condition

METACOGNITIVE AWARENESS QUESTIONNAIRE

Name:	Class:

Please answer all questions on this questionnaire.

Please answer the question with respect to the experience of receiving peer feedback on your Inspiration assignment.

- The activity of receiving peer feedback changed my perspective of the value of peer assessment.

    Strongly disagree   Disagree   Neutral   Agree   Strongly agree

    o Why or Why not?

Please answer all questions with respect to the experience of revising your Inspiration assignment. (Please circle one answer for each statement)

1. I thought about what I really needed to learn before I revised my Inspiration assignment.

    Strongly disagree   Disagree   Neutral   Agree   Strongly agree

2. I created my own examples to make information more meaningful when I revised my Inspiration assignment.

    Strongly disagree   Disagree   Neutral   Agree   Strongly agree

3. I asked myself periodically if I was meeting my goals while I revised my Inspiration assignment.

    Strongly disagree   Disagree   Neutral   Agree   Strongly agree

4. I asked others for help when I don't understand something about the revision of Inspiration assignment.

    Strongly disagree   Disagree   Neutral   Agree   Strongly agree

5. I summarized what I'd learned after I finished revising my Inspiration assignment.

    Strongly disagree   Disagree   Neutral   Agree   Strongly agree

6. I set specific goals before I began revising my Inspiration assignment.

    Strongly disagree   Disagree   Neutral   Agree   Strongly agree

7. I drew pictures or diagrams to help me understand while I revised my Inspiration assignment.

    Strongly disagree   Disagree   Neutral   Agree   Strongly agree

8. I asked myself if I had considered all options when revising my Inspiration assignment.

    Strongly disagree   Disagree   Neutral   Agree   Strongly agree

9. I stopped and went back over new information that was not clear during the revision of my Inspiration assignment.

    Strongly disagree   Disagree   Neutral   Agree   Strongly agree

Thank you!

For Assessee's role condition

10. I asked myself how well I'd accomplished my goals once I finished revising my Inspiration assignment.

Strongly disagree	Disagree	Neutral	Agree	Strongly agree

11. I asked myself about the Inspiration assignment before I began revising.

Strongly disagree	Disagree	Neutral	Agree	Strongly agree

12. I focused on overall meaning rather than specifics when I revised my Inspiration assignment.

Strongly disagree	Disagree	Neutral	Agree	Strongly agree

13. I asked myself questions about how well I was doing while I was revising my Inspiration assignment.

Strongly disagree	Disagree	Neutral	Agree	Strongly agree

14. I stopped and reread when I got confused in Inspiration assignment revision.

Strongly disagree	Disagree	Neutral	Agree	Strongly agree

15. I asked myself if I had learned as much as I could have once I finished revising my Inspiration assignment.

Strongly disagree	Disagree	Neutral	Agree	Strongly agree

Thank you!

For Both roles condition

METACOGNITIVE AWARENESS QUESTIONNAIRE

Name:	Class:

Please answer all questions on this questionnaire.

Please answer the question with respect to your experience of peer assessment on Inspiration assignment.

- The activity of peer assessment changed my perspective of the value of peer assessment.   Strongly disagree   Disagree   Neutral   Agree   Strongly agree

     o   Why or Why not?

Please answer all questions with respect to the experience of revising your Inspiration assignment. (Please circle one answer for each statement)

1. I thought about what I really needed to learn before I revised my Inspiration assignment.   Strongly disagree   Disagree   Neutral   Agree   Strongly agree

2. I created my own examples to make information more meaningful when I revised my Inspiration assignment.   Strongly disagree   Disagree   Neutral   Agree   Strongly agree

3. I asked myself periodically if I was meeting my goals while I revised my Inspiration assignment.   Strongly disagree   Disagree   Neutral   Agree   Strongly agree

4. I asked others for help when I don't understand something about the revision of Inspiration assignment.   Strongly disagree   Disagree   Neutral   Agree   Strongly agree

5. I summarized what I'd learned after I finished revising my Inspiration assignment.   Strongly disagree   Disagree   Neutral   Agree   Strongly agree

6. I set specific goals before I began revising my Inspiration assignment.   Strongly disagree   Disagree   Neutral   Agree   Strongly agree

7. I drew pictures or diagrams to help me understand while I revised my Inspiration assignment.   Strongly disagree   Disagree   Neutral   Agree   Strongly agree

8. I asked myself if I had considered all options when revising my Inspiration assignment.   Strongly disagree   Disagree   Neutral   Agree   Strongly agree

9. I stopped and went back over new information that was not clear during the revision of my Inspiration assignment.   Strongly disagree   Disagree   Neutral   Agree   Strongly agree

Thank you!

For Both roles condition

10. I asked myself how well I'd accomplished my goals once I finished revising my Inspiration assignment.	Strongly disagree	Disagree	Neutral	Agree	Strongly agree
11. I asked myself about the Inspiration assignment before I began revising.	Strongly disagree	Disagree	Neutral	Agree	Strongly agree
12. I focused on overall meaning rather than specifics when I revised my Inspiration assignment.	Strongly disagree	Disagree	Neutral	Agree	Strongly agree
13. I asked myself questions about how well I was doing while I was revising my Inspiration assignment.	Strongly disagree	Disagree	Neutral	Agree	Strongly agree
14. I stopped and reread when I got confused in Inspiration assignment revision.	Strongly disagree	Disagree	Neutral	Agree	Strongly agree
15. I asked myself if I had learned as much as I could have once I finished revising my Inspiration assignment.	Strongly disagree	Disagree	Neutral	Agree	Strongly agree

Thank you!

METACOGNITIVE AWARENESS QUESTIONNAIRE

Name:	Class:

Please answer all questions on this questionnaire.

Please answer all questions with respect to the experience of revising your Inspiration assignment. (Please circle one answer for each statement)

1. I thought about what I really needed to learn before I revised my Inspiration assignment.	Strongly disagree	Disagree	Neutral	Agree	Strongly agree
2. I created my own examples to make information more meaningful when I revised my Inspiration assignment.	Strongly disagree	Disagree	Neutral	Agree	Strongly agree
3. I asked myself periodically if I was meeting my goals while I revised my Inspiration assignment.	Strongly disagree	Disagree	Neutral	Agree	Strongly agree
4. I asked others for help when I don't understand something about the revision of Inspiration assignment.	Strongly disagree	Disagree	Neutral	Agree	Strongly agree
5. I summarized what I'd learned after I finished revising my Inspiration assignment.	Strongly disagree	Disagree	Neutral	Agree	Strongly agree
6. I set specific goals before I began revising my Inspiration assignment.	Strongly disagree	Disagree	Neutral	Agree	Strongly agree
7. I drew pictures or diagrams to help me understand while I revised my Inspiration assignment.	Strongly disagree	Disagree	Neutral	Agree	Strongly agree
8. I asked myself if I had considered all options when revising my Inspiration assignment.	Strongly disagree	Disagree	Neutral	Agree	Strongly agree
9. I stopped and went back over new information that was not clear during the revision of my Inspiration assignment.	Strongly disagree	Disagree	Neutral	Agree	Strongly agree
10. I asked myself how well I'd accomplished my goals once I finished revising my Inspiration assignment.	Strongly disagree	Disagree	Neutral	Agree	Strongly agree
11. I asked myself about the Inspiration assignment before I began revising.	Strongly disagree	Disagree	Neutral	Agree	Strongly agree
12. I focused on overall meaning rather than specifics when I revised my Inspiration assignment.	Strongly disagree	Disagree	Neutral	Agree	Strongly agree
13. I asked myself questions about how well I was doing while I was revising my Inspiration assignment.	Strongly disagree	Disagree	Neutral	Agree	Strongly agree

Thank you!

14. I stopped and reread when I got confused in Inspiration assignment revision.

Strongly disagree   Disagree   Neutral   Agree   Strongly agree

15. I asked myself if I had learned as much as I could have once I finished revising my Inspiration assignment.

Strongly disagree   Disagree   Neutral   Agree   Strongly agree

Thank you!

APPENDIX E
SCORING RUBRIC FOR PERFORMANCE

Scoring Rubric for Inspiration Assignment

Last four digit of SSN:		
Rater:		
1. Objective Score	**Yes (1)**	**No (0)**
Minimum 12 nodes		
Line, arrows, text in lines		
Different shapes and images		
At least one external image		
At least one web link		
Total objective score	/5	
2. Subjective score		

	Score
1. Clarity of structure	
▪ **2 point**: The concept map has a good coherent and logical structure ▪ **1 point**: Some parts are not coherent or logical, but overall the structure are understandable ▪ **0 point**: Most parts are not logical or coherent.	
2. Completeness	**Score**
▪ **2 point**: The concept map covers all of the relevant topics and issues ▪ **1 point**: Although a couple of topics and issues are missing, the concept map covers overall topic and issue ▪ **0 point**: The concept map does not cover most key topics and issues	
3. Support	**Score**
▪ **2 point**: The concept map includes an appropriate amount of supporting materials such as image and pictures ▪ **1 point**: Although the concept map does not provide enough supportive materials, the author's ideas are well supported ▪ **0 point**: The concept map provides too much or too little supportive materials	
4. Creativity	**Score**
▪ **2 point**: The concept map has a lot of unique aspects expressing author's creative ideas ▪ **1 point**: The concept map expresses the author's ideas with just a few creative aspects. ▪ **0 Point**: The concept map expresses the author's ideas in a very ordinary way	
Total subjective score:	/8

Total score:	/13

APPENDIX F

LEARNER ATTITUDE SURVEY

LEARNER ATTITUDE SURVEY

Name:	Class:

You have just finished the assignment on Inspiration (concept mapping tool).
We would like to know **how you feel about the learning experience with Inspiration**.
Please, circle one answer for each statement.

1. The Inspiration learning had very little in it that captures my attention.	Strongly agree	Agree	Neutral	Disagree	Strongly disagree
2. The things I learned in the Inspiration lesson will be useful to me.	Strongly agree	Agree	Neutral	Disagree	Strongly disagree
3. Whether or not I succeed in the Inspiration lesson was up to me.	Strongly agree	Agree	Neutral	Disagree	Strongly disagree
4. I felt that the Inspiration lesson gave me a lot of satisfaction.	Strongly agree	Agree	Neutral	Disagree	Strongly disagree
5. Instructor used an interesting variety of teaching techniques.	Strongly agree	Agree	Neutral	Disagree	Strongly disagree
6. The Inspiration lesson related to my expectations and goals.	Strongly agree	Agree	Neutral	Disagree	Strongly disagree
7. The Inspiration lesson was just too difficult for me.	Strongly agree	Agree	Neutral	Disagree	Strongly disagree
8. I enjoyed working for the Inspiration lesson.	Strongly agree	Agree	Neutral	Disagree	Strongly disagree
9. I often daydreamed while in the Inspiration lesson.	Strongly agree	Agree	Neutral	Disagree	Strongly disagree
10. The personal benefits of the Inspiration lesson were clear to me.	Strongly agree	Agree	Neutral	Disagree	Strongly disagree
11. I found the challenge level in the Inspiration lesson to be about right: neither too easy nor too hard.	Strongly agree	Agree	Neutral	Disagree	Strongly disagree
12. I felt satisfied with what I was getting from the Inspiration lesson.	Strongly agree	Agree	Neutral	Disagree	Strongly disagree
*13. There was something interesting at the beginning of the peer assessment activity that got my attention.	Strongly agree	Agree	Neutral	Disagree	Strongly disagree
*14. The peer assessment activity was relevant to my interests.	Strongly agree	Agree	Neutral	Disagree	Strongly disagree
*15. The Peer assessment activity was more difficult to understand than I would like for it to be.	Strongly agree	Agree	Neutral	Disagree	Strongly disagree
*16. Completing the peer assessment activity in the Inspiration lesson gave me a satisfying feeling of accomplishment.	Strongly agree	Agree	Neutral	Disagree	Strongly disagree

For Treatment condition

*17. The peer assessment activity had things that stimulated my curiosity.	Strongly agree	Agree	Neutral	Disagree	Strongly disagree
*18. The peer assessment activity was not relevant to my needs because I already knew most of it.	Strongly agree	Agree	Neutral	Disagree	Strongly disagree
*19. The peer assessment activity in the Inspiration lesson was too difficult.	Strongly agree	Agree	Neutral	Disagree	Strongly disagree
*20. I enjoyed the peer assessment activity so much that I would like to know more about peer assessment.	Strongly agree	Agree	Neutral	Disagree	Strongly disagree
*21. I learned some things that were surprising or unexpected.	Strongly agree	Agree	Neutral	Disagree	Strongly disagree
*22. The peer assessment activity will be useful to me.	Strongly agree	Agree	Neutral	Disagree	Strongly disagree
*23. I could not really understand quite a bit of the peer assessment activity in the Inspiration lesson.	Strongly agree	Agree	Neutral	Disagree	Strongly disagree
*24. It was a pleasure to experience on such a well-designed peer assessment.	Strongly agree	Agree	Neutral	Disagree	Strongly disagree

25. What did you like MOST about the learning experience of Inspiration?

26. What did you like LEAST about the learning experience of Inspiration?

*27. What did you like MOST about the peer assessment?

*28. What did you like LEAST about the peer assessment?

Thank you!

(*) items are additional items
that are provided only to treatment groups.

LEARNER ATTITUDE SURVEY

Name:	Class:

You have just finished the assignment on Inspiration (concept mapping tool).
We would like to know **how you feel about the learning experience with Inspiration**.
Please, circle one answer for each statement.

1. The Inspiration learning had very little in it that captures my attention.	Strongly agree	Agree	Neutral	Disagree	Strongly disagree
2. The things I learned in the Inspiration lesson will be useful to me.	Strongly agree	Agree	Neutral	Disagree	Strongly disagree
3. Whether or not I succeed in the Inspiration lesson was up to me.	Strongly agree	Agree	Neutral	Disagree	Strongly disagree
4. I felt that the Inspiration lesson gave me a lot of satisfaction.	Strongly agree	Agree	Neutral	Disagree	Strongly disagree
5. Instructor used an interesting variety of teaching techniques.	Strongly agree	Agree	Neutral	Disagree	Strongly disagree
6. The Inspiration lesson related to my expectations and goals.	Strongly agree	Agree	Neutral	Disagree	Strongly disagree
7. The Inspiration lesson was just too difficult for me.	Strongly agree	Agree	Neutral	Disagree	Strongly disagree
8. I enjoyed working for the Inspiration lesson.	Strongly agree	Agree	Neutral	Disagree	Strongly disagree
9. I often daydreamed while in the Inspiration lesson.	Strongly agree	Agree	Neutral	Disagree	Strongly disagree
10. The personal benefits of the Inspiration lesson were clear to me.	Strongly agree	Agree	Neutral	Disagree	Strongly disagree
11. I found the challenge level in the Inspiration lesson to be about right: neither too easy nor too hard.	Strongly agree	Agree	Neutral	Disagree	Strongly disagree
12. I felt satisfied with what I was getting from the Inspiration lesson.	Strongly agree	Agree	Neutral	Disagree	Strongly disagree

13. What did you like MOST about the learning experience of Inspiration?

14. What did you like LEAST about the learning experience of Inspiration?

Thank You!

APPENDIX G

DEMOGRAPHIC INFORMATION SURVEY

DEMOGRAPHIC INFORMATION SURVEY

Demographic Information

1. **Name**
   (Info. for tracking only)

2. **Section**

3. **Age**

4. **Gender**

5. **Major**

6. **What year are you in school?**

   (Circle one) 1) Freshman, 2) Sophomore, 3) Junior, 4) Senior

7. **What is your ethnicity?**

   (Circle one) 1) Caucasian, 2) Asian, 3) Hispanic, 4) African

   American, 5) Other_____

APPENDIX H

PRIOR METACOGNITIVE AWARENESS SURVEY

PRIOR METACOGNITIVE AWARENESS SURVEY

Metacognitive Awareness (Circle one answer for each statement)

1. I set specific goals before I begin a task.	Strongly disagree	Disagree	Neutral	Agree	Strongly agree
2. I consciously focus my attention on important information.	Strongly disagree	Disagree	Neutral	Agree	Strongly agree
3. I ask myself questions about how well I am doing while I am learning something new.	Strongly disagree	Disagree	Neutral	Agree	Strongly agree
4. I ask others for help when I don't understand something.	Strongly disagree	Disagree	Neutral	Agree	Strongly agree
5. I ask myself if I learned as much as I could have once I finish a task.	Strongly disagree	Disagree	Neutral	Agree	Strongly agree

APPENDIX I

PRIOR ATTITUDE SURVEY

PRIOR ATTITUDE SURVEY

Course Interest (Circle one answer for each statement)					
1. My curiosity is often stimulated by the questions asked or the problems given on the subject matter in this class.	Strongly disagree	Disagree	Neutral	Agree	Strongly agree
2. The things I am learning in this course will be useful to me.	Strongly disagree	Disagree	Neutral	Agree	Strongly agree
3. I feel confident that I will do well in this course.	Strongly disagree	Disagree	Neutral	Agree	Strongly agree
4. I feel satisfied with what I am getting from this course.	Strongly disagree	Disagree	Neutral	Agree	Strongly agree

APPENDIX J

HUMAN SUBJECT COMMITTEE APPROVAL

Florida State
UNIVERSITY

Office of the Vice President For Research
Human Subjects Committee
Tallahassee, Florida 32306-2763
(850) 644-8673 · FAX (850) 644-4392

APPROVAL MEMORANDUM

Date: 10/11/2004

To:
Minjeong Kim
1951 N. Meridian Rd #85
Tallahassee, FL 32303

Dept.: EDUCATIONAL PSYCHOLOGY AND LEARNING SYSTEMS

From: **John Tomkowiak, Chair**

Re: **Use of Human Subjects in Research**
    The effects of different types of learner's role (assessor's role and assessee's role) on
performance, attitude, and metacognitive awareness in preservice teachers' technology related
project

The forms that you submitted to this office in regard to the use of human subjects in the proposal
referenced above have been reviewed by the Secretary, the Chair, and two members of the Human
Subjects Committee. Your project is determined to be Exempt per 45 CFR § 46.101(b) 2 and has been
approved by an accelerated review process.

The Human Subjects Committee has not evaluated your proposal for scientific merit, except to
weigh the risk to the human participants and the aspects of the proposal related to potential
risk and benefit. This approval does not replace any departmental or other approvals, which
may be required.

If the project has not been completed by **10/10/2005** you must request renewed approval for
continuation of the project.

You are advised that any change in protocol in this project must be approved by resubmission of the
project to the Committee for approval. Also, the principal investigator must promptly report, in writing,
any unexpected problems causing risks to research subjects or others.

By copy of this memorandum, the chairman of your department and/or your major professor is
reminded that he/she is responsible for being informed concerning research projects involving human
subjects in the department, and should review protocols of such investigations as often as needed to
insure that the project is being conducted in compliance with our institution and with DHHS regulations.

This institution has an Assurance on file with the Office for Protection from Research Risks. The
Assurance Number is IRB00000446.

Cc: Amy Baylor
HSC No. 2004.656

136

Informed Consent Form

Dear Student,

You are invited to participate in a study of peer assessment. I am a graduate student under the direction of Professor Amy Baylor in the College of Education at Florida State University.

I am conducting a research study to know the effects of assessor's role and assessee's role on performance, attitude, and metacognitive awareness in preservice teachers' technology-related project. You were selected as a possible participant in this study because you registered for EME 2040 (Introduction to Educational Technology) that teaches preservice teachers how to use technology for their instruction and professional development.

If you decide to participate, the data will be collected from you in the following activities. During week 13 to 14 (lesson for Inspiration) of the EME 2040 course, you will participate concept mapping activities and peer assessment activities (only for treatment group). First, you will submit your draft version of concept map assignment. Then, you will have an opportunity of peer assessment. Finally, you will elaborate or revise the concept map on the basis of peer assessment experience.

All students enrolled in EME 2040 will be expected to participate in the concept mapping activity (submit a draft assignment at week 13 & submit revised final assignment at week 14) as a regular part of the course. However, those who give their consent to participate in the research study will be asked to engage in the following additional activities: assess peer's draft & receive feedback. It will take about 30 minutes. In addition, the researcher will conduct two surveys to collect participants' metacognitive awareness and attitude data after finishing the activities. Estimated time to complete the two surveys is about 20 minutes. Revised assignment will be scored by researcher for the purpose of this study not for the course grade. However, revised assignment will be scored separately by instructor for the course grade purpose because it is a regular part of the course.

Any information that is obtained in connection with this study and that can be identified will remain confidential to the extent allowed by law and will not be disclosed. All the data collected will be stored in a locked cabinet at the researcher's home and will be accessed and used only for research purposes. All data will be destroyed by December 31, 2004.

Your decision whether or not to participate will not prejudice your final grade in EME 2040. If you decide to participate, you will be offered a copy of this form to keep and you are free to discontinue participation at any time without prejudice. If you have any questions, please ask me. If you have additional questions later, contact Minjeong Kim at mmk2901@garnet.acns.fsu.edu or Dr. Amy Baylor at 850-644-5203. We will be happy to answer them. If you have any questions about your rights as a subject/participant in this research, or if you feel you have been placed at risk, you can contact the Chair of the Human Subjects Committee, Institutional Review Board, through the Vice President for the Office of Research at (850) 644-8633.

You are making a decision whether or not to participate. Your signature indicates that you have read the information provided above and have decided to participate. You may withdraw at any time without prejudice after signing this form should you choose to discontinue participation in this study.

Sincerely,

Minjeong Kim

I voluntarily agree to participate in the study. I grant permission for the concept map assignment and peer assessment activities to be used only by Minjeong Kim for analysis of the data. I grant permission for the data generated from the above methods to be published in the dissertation and future publication(s).

Print name)_____

Signature_____ Date_____

APPENDIX K

COPYRIGHT PERMISSION

COPYRIGHT PERMISSION

Dear Dr. Keller,

I am writing a dissertation at Florida State University entitled "The effects of Assessor's role and Assessee's role on metacognitive awareness, performance, and attitude in computer-related design task." I would like your permission to reprint your copyrighted materials in my dissertation. The copyrighted materials are:

Keller, J. (1987) Course Interest Survey
Keller, J. (1993) Instructional Materials Motivation Survey

The requested permission extends to any future revisions and editions of my dissertation, including non-exclusive world rights in all languages. These rights will in no way restrict republication of the material in any other form by you or by others authorized by you. This authorization is extended to University Microfilms International (UMI), Ann Arbor, Michigan, for the purpose of reproducing and distributing copies of this dissertation. Your signing of this letter will also confirm that you own the copyright to the above-described material.

If these arrangements meet with your approval, please sign this letter where indicated below and return it to me in the enclosed return envelope. Thank you very much.

Best regards,

Minjeong Kim

PERMISSION GRANTED FOR THE USE REQUESTED ABOVE:

Dr. John Keller

REFERENCES

Ballantyne, R., Hughies, K., & Mylonas, A. (2002). Developing procedures for implementing peer assessment in large classes using an action research process. *Assessment and Evaluation in Higher Education, 27*(5), 427-441.

Bangert, A. W. (1995). *Peer assessment: an instructional strategy for effectively implementing performance-based assessments.* University of South Dakota, Vermillion.

Bangert-Drowns, R. L., Kulik, C.-L. C., Kulik, J. A., & Morgan, M. (1991). The instructional effects of feedback in test-like events. *Review of Educational Research, 61*(2), 213-238.

Blom, D., & Poole, K. (2004). Peer assessment of tertiary music performance: opportunities for understanding performance assessment and performing through experience and self-reflection. *British Journal of Music Education, 21*(1), 111-125.

Bloxham, S., & West, A. (2004). Understanding the rules of the game: marking peer assessment as a medium for developing students' conceptions of assessment. *Assessment and Evaluation in Higher Education, 29*(6), 721-733.

Boud, D. (1990). Assessment and the promotion of academic values. *Studies in Higher Education, 15*, 101-111.

Boud, D. (1995). *Enhancing learning through self-assessment.* London: Kogan Page.

Brindley, C., & Scoffield, S. (1998). Peer assessment in undergraduate programmes. *Teaching in higher education, 3*(1), 79-89.

Brown, S., & Knight, P. (1994). *Assessing learners in higher education.* London: Kogan Page.

Brufee, K. A. (1985). *A short course in writing: Practical rhetoric for teaching composition through collaborative learning* (3rd ed.). Boston, MA: Little.

Butcher, A. C., Stefani, L. A. J., & Tariq, V. N. (1995). Analysis of peer-, self-, and staff-assessment in group project work. *Assessment in Education, 2*(2), 165-185.

Butler, D. L., & Winne, P. H. (1995). Feedback and self-regulated learning: A theoretical synthesis. *Review of Educational Research, 65*, 245-281.

Cheng, W., & Warren, M. (1997). Having sceond thoughts: Student perceptions before and after a peer assessment exercise. *Studies in Higher Education, 22*(2), 233-240.

Chi, M. T. H. (1996). Constructing self-explanations and scaffolded explanations in tutoring. *Applied Cognitive Psychology, 10*, 33-49.

Cohen, J. (1988). *Staistical power analysis for the behavioral sciences* (2nd ed.). Hillsdale,NJ: Elrbaum.

141

Csikszentmihalyi, M. (1978). Instrinsic rewards and emergent motiation. In M. R. Lepper & D. Greene (Eds.), *The hidden costs of reward* (pp. 205-216). Hillsdale, NJ: Lawrence Erlbaum Associates.

Daniel, R. (2004). Peer assessment in musical performance: the development, trial and evaluation of a methodology for the Australian tertiary environment. *British Journal of Music Education, 21*(1), 89-110.

Devenney, R. (1989). How ESL teachers and peers evaluate and respond to student writing. *URELC Journal: A Journal of Language Teaching and Research in Southeast Asia, 20,* 77-90.

Dochy, F., Segers, M., & Sluijsmans, D. M. A. (1999). The use of self-, peer and co-assessment in higher education: A review. *Studies in Higher Education, 24*(3), 331-350.

Dweck, C. S. (1975). The role of expectations and attributions in the alleviation of learned helplessness. *Journal of Personality and Social Psychology, 31,* 674-685.

Ewers, T., & Searby, M. (1997). Peer assessment in music. *The new academic, 6*(2), 5-7.

Falchikov, N. (1995). Peer feedback marking: developing peer assessment. *Innovations in Education and Training International, 32*(2), 175-187.

Falchikov, N. (2003). *Learning Together:peer tutoring in higher education.* London, New York: Routledge.

Freeman, M. (1995). Peer assessment by groups of group work. *Assessment and Evaluation in Higher Education, 20*(3), 289-300.

Garcia, T., & Pintrich, R. (1991). *Student motivation and self-regulated learning: A LISREL model.* Paper presented at the AERA, Chicago, IL.

Gartner, A., Kohler, M., & Riessman, F. (1971). *Children teach children: learning by teaching.* New York: Harper and Row.

Gayo-Avello, D., & Fernandes-Cuervo, H. (2003). *Online self-assessment as a learning method.* Paper presented at the IEEE International Conference on Advanced Learning Technologies (ICALT' 03).

Goodlad, S., & Hirst, B. (1989). *Peer tutoring: a guide to learning by teaching.* New York: Nichold Publishing.

Higgins, L., Flower, L., & Petraglia, J. (1992). Planning text together: The role of critical reflection in student collaboration. *Journal of Educational Psychology, 71*(5), 605.

Hunter, D., & Russ, M. (1996). Peer assessment in performance studies. *British Journal of Music Education, 13,* 67-78.

Johnson, D. W., Johnson, R. T., & Holubec, E. J. (1991). *Cooperation in the classroom.* Edina, MN: Interaction Book Co.

Johnson, R. (1999). Helping students to understand and use assessment for learning. In S. Avery, C. Bryan & G. Wisker (Eds.), *Innovations in teaching English and textual studies* (pp. 181-197): SEDA paper.

Kafai, Y., & Resnick, M. (1996). *Constructionism in practice: designing, thinking, and learning in a digital world.* Mahwah, NJ: Lawrence Erlbaum Associates.

Keig, L. (2000). Formative peer review of teaching: attitudes of faculty at liberal arts colleges toward colleague assessment. *Journal of Personnel Evaluation in Education, 14*(1), 67-87.

Keller, J. M. (1987). Course Interest Survey.

Keller, J. M. (1993). Instructional Materials Motivation Survey.

142

Kim, M. (2003). *Peer assessment as a learning method: Various assessment criteria for students with different self-regulation levels.* Paper presented at the AECT, Anaheim, CA.

Kim, M. (2004). *Why online peer assessment is needed?* Paper presented at the AECT, Chicago, IL.

Kim, M., & Ryu, J. (2004). *Instrument validation study: Revised CIS, IMMS, & MAI.*Unpublished manuscript.

Kirk, R. E. (1982). *Experimental design: procedures for the behavioral sciences.* Monterey, Calif.: Books/Cole Pub. Co.

Lejk, M., & Wyvill, M. (2001). the effect of the inclusion of self-assessment with peer assessment of contributions to a group project: a quantitative study of secret and agreed assessments. *Assessment and Evaluation in Higher Education, 26*(6), 551-561.

Lin, S. S. J., Liu, E. Z. F., & Yuan, S. M. (2001). Web-based peer assessment: feedback for student with various thinking-styles. *Journal of Computer Assisted Learning, 17,* 420-432.

Lynch, D. H., & Golen, S. (1992). Peer evaluation of writing in business communication classes. *Journal of Education for Business, Sept/Oct,* 44-48.

McDowell, L. (1995). The impact of innovative assessment on student learning. *Innovations in Education and Training International, 32,* 302-313.

McLuckie, J., & Topping, K. J. (2004). Transferable skills for online peer learning. *Assessment and Evaluation in Higher Education, 29*(5), 563-584.

Miller, P. J. (2003). The effect of coring criteria specificity on peer and self-assessment. *Assessment and Evaluation in Higher Education, 28*(4), 383-393.

Mowl, G., & Pain, R. (1995). Using self and peer assessment to improve students' essay writing: a case study from geography. *Innovations in Education and Training International, 32,* 324-335.

O'Donnell, A. M., Larson, C. O., Dansereau, D. F., & Rocklin, T. R. (1986). Effects of cooperation and editing on instruction qriting performance. *Journal of Experimental Education, 54,* 207-210.

Oldfield, K. A., & MacAlpine, M. K. (1995). Peer and self assessment at tertiary level-an experiential report. *Assessment and Evaluation in Higher Education, 20*(1), 125-132.

Orsmond, P., Merry, S., & Reiling, K. (1996). The importance of marking criteria in the use of peer assessment. *Assessment and Evaluation in Higher Education, 21*(3), 239-249.

Orsmond, P., Merry, S., & Reiling, K. (2000). The use of student derived marking criteria in peer and self-assessment. *Assessment and Evaluation in Higher Education, 25*(1), 23-38.

Orsmond, P., Merry, S., & Reiling, K. (2002). The use of examplars and formative feedback when using student derived marking criteria in peer and self-assessment. *Assessment and Evaluation in Higher Education, 27*(4), 309-323.

Panitz, T. (1997). Collaborative versus cooperative learning: comparing the two definitions helps understand the nature of interactive learning. *Cooperative Learning and College Teaching, 8*(2).

Papert, S. (1993). *The children's machine: Rethinking school in the age of the computer.* New York: Basic Books.

Paris, S. G., & Newman, R. S. (1990). Developmental aspects of self-regulated learning. *Educational Psychologist, 25,* 87-102.

Purchase, H. C. (2000). Learning about interfacedesign through peer assessment. *Assessment and Evaluation in Higher Education, 27*(4), 341-352.

Race, P. (1998). Practical pointers in peer assessment. In S. Brown (Ed.), *Peer Assessment in Practice*. Brimingham: SEDA.

Rada, R., Acquah, S., Baker, B., & Ramsey, P. (1993). Collaborative learning and the MUCH system. *Computers & Education, 20*, 225-233.

Resnick, M., Bruckman, A., & Martin, F. (1996). Pianos not stereos: Creating computational construction kits. *Interactions, 3*(6).

Rushton, C., Ramsey, P., & Rada, R. (1993). Peer assessment in a collaborative hypermedia environment: A case study. *Journal of Computer-Based Instruction, 20*(3), 73-80.

Rust, C., Price, M., & O'Donovan, B. (2003). Improving students' learning by developing their understanding of assessment criteria and processes. *Assessment and Evaluation in Higher Education, 28*(2), 147-164.

Schneider, T. (2001). Analysis of incomplete climate data: Estimation of mean values and covariance matrices and imputation of missing values. *Journal of Climate, 14*, 853-871.

Schraw, G., & Dennison, R. S. (1994). Assessing metacognitive awareness. *Contemporary Educational Psychology, 19*, 460-475.

Searby, M., & Ewers, T. (1997). An evaluation of the use of peer assessment in higher education: A case study in school of Music, Kingston University. *Assessment and Evaluation in Higher Education, 22*(4), 371-383.

Sluijsmans, D. M. A., Brand-Gruwel, S., & vanMerrienboer, J. J. G. (2002). Peer assessment training in teacher education: effects on performance and perceptions. *Assessment and Evaluation in Higher Education, 27*(5), 443-454.

Sluijsmans, D. M. A., Brand-Gruwel, S., vanMerrienboer, J. J. G., & Bastiens, T. J. (2003). The training of peer assessment skills to promote the development of reflection skills in teacher education. *Studies in Educational Evaluation, 29*, 23-42.

Smyth, K. (2004). The benefits of students learning about critical evaluation rather than being summatively judged. *Assessment and Evaluation in Higher Education, 29*(3), 369-378.

Staphani, L. A. J. (1998). Assessment in partnership with learners. *Assessment and Evaluation in Higher Education, 23*(4), 339-350.

Stevens, J. (1996). *Applied multivariate statistics for the social sciences (3rd ed.)*. Hillsdale, N.J.: Lawrence Erlbaum.

Strachan, I. B., & Wilcox, S. (1996). Peer and self assessment of group work; Developing an effective response to increased enrollment in a third-year course in microclimatology. *Journal of Geography in Higher Education, 20*, 343-353.

Topping, K. (1998). Peer assessment between students in colleges and universities. *Review of Educational Research, 68*(3), 249-276.

Topping, K., & Ehly, S. (1998). *Peer assisted learning*. Mahwah, NJ: Lawrence Erlbaum Associates.

Topping, K., Smith, F. F., Swanson, I., & Elliot, A. (2000). Formative peer assessment of academic writing between postgraduate students. *Assessment and Evaluation in Higher Education, 25*(2), 149-169.

Tower, L., & Broadfoot, P. (1992). Self-assessment in the primary school. *Educational Review, 44*(2), 137-151.

Tsai, C.-C., Lin, S. S. J., & Yhan, S.-M. (2002). Developing science activities through a networked peer assessment system. *Computers & Education, 38*, 241-252.

Van Lehn, K. A., Chi, M. T. H., Baggett, W., & Murray, R. C. (1995). *Progress report: Towards a theory of learning during tutoring*. Pittsburgh,PA: Learning Research and Development Center, University of Pittsburgh.

Vygotsky, L. S., Cole, M., John-Steiner, V., Scribner, S., & Souberman, E. (1978). *Mind in society*. Cambridge, MA: Harvard University Press.

Woolf, H. (2004). Assessment criteria: reflections on current practices. *Assessment and Evaluation in Higher Education, 29*(4), 479-493.

Zimmerman, B. J. (1990). Self-regulated learning and academic achivement;An overview. *Educational Psychologist, 25*, 3-17.

Zimmerman, B. J., Greenberg, D., & Weinstein, C. E. (1994). Self-regulateing academic study time: A strategy approach. In D. Schunk & B. Zimmerman (Eds.), *Self-regulation of learning and performance: Issues and educational applications* (pp. 181-199). Hillsdale, NJ: Lawrence Erlbaum Associates.

BIOGRAPHICAL SKETCH

(Minjeong Kim)

Date of Birth: June, 9. 1972

Education
- Florida State University, Tallahassee, Florida (Fall, 2001 – Summer, 2005)
  Doctoral Program, Instructional Systems
- Hanyang University, Seoul, Korea (Fall, 1997 – Spring, 1999)
  M.A., Educational Technology
- Hanyang University, Seoul, Korea (Spring, 1991 – Fall, 1995)
  B.A., Educational Foundations

Certificate
- **Certificate of Measurement and Statistics** by Department of Educational Psychology and Learning Systems, Florida State University, Tallahassee, Florida. (in request)
- **Certificate of Program Evaluation** by Department of Educational Psychology and Learning Systems, Florida State University, Tallahassee, Florida. (in request)
- **Certificate of Education Teacher for Secondary Education** by Minister of Education, Seoul, Korea.
- **Certificate of English Teacher for Secondary Education** by Minister of Education, Seoul, Korea.
- **Certificate of Specialist for life-long education** by Minister of Education, Seoul, KoreaCertificate of Measurement and Statistics by Department of Educational Psychology and Learning Systems, Florida State University, Tallahassee, Florida.

Honor/Award
- **University Dissertation Grant Award** (spring, 2005)
- **Excellent International Student Award** of Instructional Systems in the Department of Educational Psychology and Learning Systems (2004 - 2005) by Gagne/Briggs Foundation, Florida State University.
- **Finalist of the Outstanding Doctoral Student Award** of Instructional Systems in the Department of Educational Psychology and Learning Systems (2004 - 2005) by Gagne/Briggs Foundation, Florida State University.

- **Finalist of the Future Professor Award** of Instructional Systems in the Department of Educational Psychology and Learning Systems (2004 - 2005) by Gagne/Briggs Foundation, Florida State University.
- **Finalist of the Excellent International Student Award** of Instructional Systems in the Department of Educational Psychology and Learning Systems (2003 - 2004) by Gagne/Briggs Foundation, Florida State University.
- **Finalist of the Future Professor Award** of Instructional Systems in the Department of Educational Psychology and Learning Systems (2003 - 2004) by Gagne/Briggs Foundation, Florida State University.
- **Co-recipient of AECT's 2003 Service Award**: PT3 project awarded by Association for Educational Communications and Technology
- **Award of the Outstanding Student** of College of Education (1995), Hanyang University in Korea.

Employment/Work Experience
- **Learning Systems Institute (LSI)**
  - * Florida State University, Tallahassee, Florida
  - * (Jan./2003 – Aug./2005) **Graduate Assistant**
  - * Research and development of the statewide project, Accommodation and Modification for students with Disabilities
  - * Design, development, and evaluation of EPSS for special education teacher's instructional planning
- **Korea Banking Institute (KBI),** Seoul, Korea
  - * (June. 2005) **Delegation Leader and coordinator** for the American Society for Training and Development (ASTD) in Washington D.C
  - * (May. 2004) **Delegation Leader and coordinator** for the American Society for Training and Development (ASTD) in Orlando, FL.
- **PT 3 project of AECT**
  - * (10/2001 -5/2002) **Graduate Assistant**
  - * Developing exemplary practice of technology use of teachers
- **Korea Education & Research Information Service (KERIS)**
  - * (8/2001-12/2001) **Information consultant** for ICT trends and issues of other countries (part-time)
  - * (1/1999-6/1999) **Web-based course designer** - Designing and evaluating the Electronic textbooks for elementary students (part-time)
- **Hanyang University**
  - * Department of Educational Technology
  - * (1/1998-12/1998) **Teaching Assistant** for Computer Based Instruction Lab
- **Samsung SDS multicampus**
  - * E-learning division of Samsung company
  - * (9/1997-12/1997) **Training course designer and consultant** for Performance system analysis (part-time)
- **Korean Federation of Teachers' Association**
  - * (2/1995-8/1997) full-time
  - * **Chief Secretary** of president

Publications

<u>Book Chapter</u>
- Kim, D. & Kim, M. (1998). Instructional Design Automation, Trends and Issues in Educational Technology. Pubisher: Kyo-uk Koa-Hak Sa Inc, Seoul, Korea. (In Korean)

<u>Articles in Referred Proceedings</u>
- Kim, M. (2005). Learning by assessing, Proceeding of annual conference of American Educational Research Association (2005 AERA), Montreal, Canada.
- Kim, M., Lee, M. & Park, S. (2004) Potential Areas in Calculating Return On Investment for E-learning: An investigation through case studies, Proceeding of World Conference on E-Learning in Corporate, Government, Healthcare, & Higher Education (E-LEARN 2004), Washington, D.C.
- Lee, Y., Son,C. & Kim,M. (2004) Preliminary Analysis of Evaluation Criteria in E-Learning Return On Investment (ROI), Proceeding of World Conference on E-Learning in Corporate, Government, Healthcare, & Higher Education (E-LEARN, 2004), Washington, D.C.
- Lee, M., Park, S. & Kim, M. (2004) Finding Return On Investment Factors in E-Learning, Proceeding of World Conference on E-Learning in Corporate, Government, Healthcare, & Higher Education (E-LEARN, 2004), Washington, D.C.
- Park, S., Kim, M, & Ryu, J. (2004) Searching for Optimized ROI Process for E-Learning, Proceeding of world Conference on E-Learning in Corporate, Government, Healthcare, & Higher Education (E-LEARN, 2004), Washington, D.C.
- Kim, M. & Beech, M. (2004) Evaluation on the effectiveness of EPSS: A case study. Proceeding of annual conference of Association for Educational Communications & Technology (AECT), Chicago, Illinois.
- Kim, M. (2004) Why web-based peer assessment is needed? Proceeding of annual conference of Association for Educational Communications & Technology (AECT), Chicago, Illinois.
- Son, C., Kim, M., Oh, S. & Caplini, R. (2004) Performance systems analysis: How to facilitate innovations in an organization. Proceeding of annual conference of Association for Educational Communications & Technology (AECT), Chicago, Illinois.
- Kim, M. & Ryu, J. (2004) Designing adaptive learning objects based on learner's knowledge status, Proceeding of annual conference of Association for Educational Communications & Technology (AECT), Chicago, Illinois.
- Beech, M. & Kim, M. (2004) Demonstration of Instruction Manage 2: An instructional planning tool for special education teachers, Proceeding of World Conference on Society for Information Technology & Teacher Education (SITE), Atlanta, Georgia.
- Kim, M. (2004) Developing an Instructional Planning Tool for Special Education Teachers, Proceeding of World Conference on Society for Information Technology & Teacher Education (SITE), Atlanta, Georgia.
- Son, C., Kim, M. & Park, S. (2004) Handheld Computers Approaching Classrooms: Instructional Guidelines for Teaching and Leaning with Handheld Computers, Proceeding of World Conference on Society for Information Technology & Teacher Education (SITE), Atlanta, Georgia.

- Kim, M. & Beech, M. (2003) Usability test for Electronic Performance Support System: Developing an instructional planning tool for special education teachers, Proceeding of World Conference on E-Learning in Corporate, Government, Healthcare, & Higher Education (E-LEARN), Phoenix, Arizona.
- Ryu, J., Oh, S. & Kim, M. (2003) Designing adaptive learning objects, Proceeding of World Conference on E-Learning in Corporate, Government, Healthcare, & Higher Education (E-LEARN), Phoenix, Arizona.
- Park, S., Kim, M., & Ryu, J. (2003) The Effect of character spacing on reading in Personal Digital Assistant (PDA), Proceeding of World Conference on E-Learning in Corporate, Government, Healthcare, & Higher Education (E-LEARN), Phoenix, Arizona.
- Kim, M (2003). Peer assessment as a learning method: various assessment formats for students with different self-regulation level. Proceeding of annual conference of Association for Educational Communications & Technology (AECT), Anaheim, California.
- Kim, M., & Ryu, J. (2003). Meta-analysis of the effectiveness of pedagogical agent, Proceeding of World Conference on Educational Multimedia, Hypermedia & Telecommunication (ED-MEDIA), Honolulu, Hawaii.

Technical Report
- Beech, M., Nalon, S., Nalon, J & Kim, M. (2003). The ESE Instruction Manager 2 User's Guide and Tutorial, Project of Accommodations and Modifications, Learning System Institute, Florida State University

Master Thesis
- Kim, M. (1999). The effectiveness of metacognitive button on learning achievement in web-based learning. Masters Dissertation, Hanyang University, Korea.

Instructional Production
- The ESE Instructional Manager 2: Instructional planning tool for special education teachers (1/2003-4/2004)
- The tutorial for the ESE Instruction Manager 2 (9/2003-5/2004)
- The online tutorial for the ESE Instruction Manager 2 (1/2004-11/2004)

Above three instrutional products are Project products of Accommodation and Modification for Students with disabilities in the Learning System Institute (LSI), Florida State University, Tallahassee, FL (Funded by Bureau of Instructional Support and Community Service, Florida Department of Education) (Reference: Dr. Beech, project manager (mbeech@lsi.fsu.edu))

Service to the Profession
- **American Educational Research Association (AERA)**
  * Graduate student Liaison (2003-present)
  * Proposal reviewer for 2004, 2005 conference
- **Association for the Advancement of Computer in Education (AACE)**
  * Student volunteer and session chair in various conferences under AACE (ED-Media 2003, E-learn 2003, SITE 2004)
  * Proposal reviewer for the International Journal of E-learning(IJEL)

- <u>**American Educational Communication and Technology (AECT)**</u>
  - *   Proposal reviewer for 2004, 2005 conference

Service to the Community
- Korean Catholic Community in Tallahassee, FL
  - *   Treasurer (2001-2005)

Competencies
- **Computer Skills:** Intermediate User of Photoshop, File Maker Pro, and Dreamweaver. Advance User of SPSS, LISREL, Toolbook, and Web-applications.
- **Statistical Skills:** ANOVA, ANCOVA, MANOVA, MANCOVA, Structural Equation Model, Regression, Correspondence Analysis, Cluster Analysis, Factor Analysis, Meta-analysis, Non-parametric Analysis, and etc.
- **Research Methodology Courses:** Methods in Educational Research, Experimental Design, General Linear Model, Practicum in Experimental Learning Research, Assessment of Learning Outcome, Qualitative Methods in Evaluation, Advanced Topic of Analysis Variance, Non-parametric Analysis, Scale and Instrument Development, and Multivariate Analysis